To: Sean + Paul.
August 2000

From Grandma + Grandpa

Chinese Wushu Series

Basics of
Taiji Quan

Li Xingdong

FOREIGN LANGUAGES PRESS   BEIJING

First Edition   1995
Second Printing   1998

ISBN 7-119-00171-X

© Foreign Languages Press, Beijing, China, 1995

Published by Foreign Languages Press
24 Baiwanzhuang Road, Beijing 100037, China

Printed by Foreign Languages Printing House
19 Chegongzhuang Xilu, Beijing 100044, China

Distributed by China International Book Trading Corporation
35 Chegongzhuang Xilu, Beijing 100044, China
P.O. Box 399, Beijing, China

Printed in the People's Republic of China

Contents

I. Origin and Development of *Taiji Quan*

Historians have traced the origins of the word "*Taiji*" to the *Book of Changes* published in the Zhou Dynasty (1100-770 B.C.). It has the meaning of supremeness, extremeness, absoluteness and soleness. *Taiji Quan* carries the same meaning. In the latter years of the 18th century, Wang Zongyue a Wushu master in Shanxi Province, wrote a book called *On Taiji Quan*, in which he applied the philosophical principles of yin and yang to explain the meaning of the art. From then on, this form was widely known as "*Taiji Quan*."

Opinions vary on the origins and founders of *Taiji Quan*. Following are some of the major explanations:

1. The Origin Can Be Traced to Chenjiagou Village

Holders of this view believe that *Taiji Quan* was founded by Chen Wangting in the late years of the Ming Dynasty (1368-1644). The chief proponents of this view are Tang Hao and Gu Liuxin, China's noted students of the history of Wushu. Mr. Tang Hao drew his conclusion after making an investigation in and around Chenjiagou Village in Wenxian County, Henan Province, where he looked up the county annals and the genealogical records of the Chen family. According to the Chen family records, Chen Wangting was "a master of the Chen-style boxing and founder of swordplay and spearplay." As the leading popular schools of *Taiji Quan* originated from or inherited from the Chen-style *Taiji Quan*, this view took on a great deal of authority and held sway for a long time.

2. *Taiji Quan* Was Founded by Zhang Sanfeng

This view was the foregone conclusion before the view stated above became popular. The *Complete Book of Taiji Quan Exercises* written by Yang Chengfu (1883-1936) says: "*Taiji Quan* was created by Zhang Sanfeng in the late years of the Song Dynasty (960-1279) and passed down by Wang Zongyue, Chen Zhoutong, Zhang Songxi and Jiang Fa, one after another." Even earlier, Li Yishe (1832-1891) wrote in his book *A Brief Note to Taiji Quan*: "*Taiji Quan* was initiated by Zhang Sanfeng in the Song Dynasty." Some people today still agree with this view.

3. *Taiji Quan* Was Founded by Wang Zongyue

Wang Zongyue, mentioned above, wrote a book called *On Taiji Quan* in which he systematically expounded the theory and techniques of *Taiji Quan*. Because the name of Wang Zongyue can be found in history books on Wushu, some people think he summed up the experiences of his predecessors to create *Taiji Quan* and then introduced it to Chenjiagou Village. The record of the historical document says, however, that: "Wang Zongyue passed *Taiji Quan* down to Jiang Fa and Jiang Fa passed it on to Chen Changxing."

4. It Was Created at Mount Wudang

Chinese Wushu is closely related to religion. It is believed that *Taiji Quan* originated in Mount Wudang, the sacred place of Taoism. Holders of this view believe that making pills of immortality was one of the major activities of ancient Chinese Taoism. The Taoist priests at Mount Wudang created *Taiji Quan* on the basis of their practical experiences in making pills of immortality (still exercises, in most cases) by combining deep breathing and physical exercises for life enhancement that guide the smooth flow of vital energy inside the body. *Taiji Quan's* main functions are to clear the channels for the energy flow and regulate the energy flow and blood so as to increase one's ability to resist illness and to prolong life. It also absorbed the strong points of other boxing styles for attack and defence.

Although the origins of *Taiji Quan* remain controversial, but the principles upon which it was founded and upon which it developed are universally accepted.

***Taiji Quan* and Chinese Classical Philosophy** *Taiji Quan*, with its peculiar characteristics, has had considerable influence on the Wushu culture of China, not only because of its functions as health preserver, martial art and temperament improver, but even more because of its profound philosophy that has aroused deep interest in practising and studying *Taiji Quan*.

The unity of opposites—negative and positive (yin and yang)—is the most fundamental thought in Chinese classical philosophy. The *Book of Changes* says that the changes in all things in the universe are the manifestations of the interaction between yin and yang. It also says that the mystical and unpredictable changes in things in the world are the inevitable outcome of the interrelationship between yin and yang. A number of concepts have thus derived from this notion. The opposites, such as motion and stillness, hard and soft, advance and retreat, open and close, flexion and extension, tension and relaxation, high and low, displayed in *Taiji Quan* are all manifestations of the changes of yin and yang. The relations between hardness and softness, stillness and motion, yin and yang, are merely an expression of the principle of unity of opposites in different forms. They are opposed to each other, but they are complementary to and interdependent upon each other. In his book *On Taiji Quan*, Wang Zongyue wrote that *Taiji Quan* is based on the changes resulting from the relations between motion and stillness, yin and yang.

"From *Wuji* to *Taiji*." The idea of "*Wuji*" (poleless) was indicated by a circle with a blank space inside in ancient China. This symbol represented the chaos (or the primeval state of the universe before the earth was first separated from the heaven, yin from yang). Embodied in *Taiji Quan*, this principle is the boxing stance in which the mind and the body are integrated in one before the movements begin, before the primeval state fraught divides into yin and yang. The *Taiji* Diagram is a circle, but as the lines of movement in *Taiji Quan* are concerned, most are planes, or small circles, big circles, ovals, semi-circles, arcs and spirals. The movements must be continuous and smooth. They are apparently bent, but actually not, or they are apparently closed, but actually not. The continuity of circles and arcs is the image of *Wuji*. Therefore, *Taiji Quan* enthusiasts must be broadminded and free from distracting thoughts. Their minds must be like the boundless universe, quiet and empty. "From *Wuji* to *Taiji*" is the fundamental notion and quintessence of *Taiji Quan*. *Taiji Quan* calls for the use of an energy stream to guide the movements of the body under the direction of the circular form. The circles include both the inner and the outer: (1) Inner circle—the flow of the energy stream should be smooth and natural; be sure not to hold the breath; (2) Outer circle—this refers to the orbit for the circular movement of the limbs and torso. Circular movements are the product of intensive research into the philosophical principles outlined in the *Book of Changes* by Chinese *Taiji Quan* masters of past dynasties. They are the quintessence of the practising method for *Taiji Quan*.

Traditional Chinese philosophy stresses the harmonious unity between Man, Nature and the universe. *Taiji Quan* has absorbed this philosophical thought. In practising the boxing, stress is laid on uprightness, relaxation, ease, comfort, slowness, softness, lightness and erectness. The essential points required for the different parts of the body are: head upright, chest drawn in, straight back, shoulders lowered, elbows down, abdomen and waist relaxed, buttocks tucked in, crotch round, knees released and light footwork. It should be noted that these points show precisely the harmonious agreement and conformity between *Taiji Quan* and Nature.

Combining *Taiji Quan* with Deep Breathing and *Dao Yin* Exercises   Deep breathing and *dao yin* exercises are Chinese health building methods with long histories. The Five-animal Play created by Hua Tuo, a noted doctor in the late years of the Han Dynasty (206 B.C.-220), combines such animal movements as shaking, stretching, jumping and looking around with breathing exercises. They are exactly the methods of *Qigong* (breathing exercises) and *Neigong* (internal exercises). The combination of the harmonious movements of the hands, eyes, body and feet with deep breathing has become *Neigong* boxing—a combination of internal energy flow and external physical exercises.

Combining Wushu with the Theory of Channels in Traditional Chinese Medicine   The channels are a special network forming part of the human body. They connect all parts of the body into an organic whole. Although no actual evidence of these channels can be found in anatomy, modern science has already proved their existence in various ways. Based on the principles of the channel theory, *Taiji Quan* routines, characterized by twining, circling and spiralling movements, are executed in curves and circles, and therefore are smooth, continuous, hard and soft. *Taiji Quan* practitioners direct their energy and strength through concentration on the different parts of their body to guide the movements. The energy stream, released from the public region, flows with the waist as axis and turns the different parts of the body gently, arms and wrists above and ankles and knees blow, before returning to the pubic region. This makes the flow of the blood and energy smooth, thus helping to cure illnesses and improve health.

The theory of *Taiji Quan* was first perfected in Wang Zongyue's book, *On Taiji Quan.* It was followed by other writings, including the *Thirteen-Form Frame, Thirteen Forms, Guide to Execution of the Thirteen Forms, Main Points for Pushing Hands, Verses to Pushing Hands, Five-Word Formula.* These works marked a more mature stage of *Taiji Quan's development.*

Taiji Quan grew quickly after the founding of the People's Republic of China. It was included in the national Wushu competition program, became a widely practised activity throughout China and took root in more than 30 other countries and regions. It was an official event at the 11th Asian Games held in Beijing in 1990.

II. Schools and Characteristics of *Taiji Quan*

Taiji Quan has developed into many schools since its emergence. Following is an introduction to the five leading schools:

1. Chen-style *Taiji Quan*

Chen-style *Taiji Quan* is divided into the old frame and the new frame. The old frame was created by Chen Wangting in the early years of the Qing Dynasty (1644-1911). It originally included five routines, (also called the thirteen forms), a set of *Chang Quan* (Long-style Boxing) consisting of 108 forms and a set of *Pao Chui* (Cannon Boxing). Based on the experience accumulated during the 300 years since Chen Wangting, Chen's originals have been improved and refined into the first two sets of the present-day Chen-style *Taiji Quan*. These sets are carefully arranged with different speeds, intensities, body techniques, amounts of physical power and degrees of difficulty, but both conform to the principles of advancing step-by-step and combining hardness with softness.

The first set consists of 83 forms. Its main features are: (1) Evident display of silk-spinning power. Make sure that in all movements, power is generated from the back and waist and carries through to the tips of the four limbs. The movements are executed in circular and spiral forms, including twining, winding, spinning and turning, so that "when one movement is executed, all parts of the body, internal and external, are moving"; (2) Combine hardness and softness, with softness dwelling in hardness. In other words, once a movement is executed, you must generate an internal strength which is apparently hard, but not hard, and apparently soft but not soft, and which is heavy and flexible; (3) The movements must be integrated with breathing and the direction of strength to make sure that the energy stream flows to the pubic region and circulates in it. Sounds can also be produced while exhaling to increase strength; (4) Equal stress on quickness and slowness. In other words, at the connections, the movements must be quick and, in general, the movements should be slow; (5) There are three frames for *Taiji Quan*, high, middle and low. Frail and unhealthy people should practise the high frame, while the young and strong should learn the low frame.

The second set was originally called *Pao Chui*, or cannon boxing, and consists of 71 forms. Its main features are: (1) There are more movements executed with power generated through foot stamping; (2) The movements are quicker and harder, and have greater explosive force than the first set; (3) There are more jumps, dodges and transfers. The second set is good for young people, but it is less popular than the first set.

The new frame of Chen-style *Taiji Quan* also has two sets. One was created by Chen Youben, a boxing teacher in Chenjiagou Village. The sequence is the same as the old frame, but its frame is smaller, the turns are also smaller and the difficult movements have been eliminated. People in the Chenjiagou Village call this Small Circle Boxing and the old frame, Big Circle Boxing. When the new set was passed on to Chen Xin, he wrote a book entitled *Illustrated Chen-style Taiji Quan* in which he dealt with the boxing experiences accumulated by the Chen family of past generations. The other set of new frame was initiated by Chen Qingping, a disciple of Chen Youben. It is characterized by compactness and slow movements. This set can be made more complicated when the practitioner has mastered the skills and practises it with more circular movements. It was first popularized in Zhaobao Township in Wenxian County, Henan Province, and is known as the Zhaobao Frame. Chen-style Boxing is the oldest and all other schools (Yang, Wu, Wu Family and Sun Style), have been developed on the basis of the Chen Style.

2. Yang-style *Taiji Quan*

The originator of Yang-style *Taiji Quan* was Yang Luchan (1800-1873), born in Yongnian County, Hebei Province. Brought up in a poor family, Yang Luchan was sold to Chen Dehu in Chenjiagou Village as a child servant. While looking after *Taiji Quan* Master Chen Changxing, Yang Luchan learned martial arts from him. He returned to his native village as an adult and began to teach *Taiji Quan* to others. People in Yongnian County described his art as "silky boxing" and "soft boxing." Later, he went to Beijing and taught many members of the nobility in the Qing Dynasty. To meet the needs of the general public, he dropped the difficult movements, such as jumps, foot stamping and force producing exercises. Yang's son revised this form into the Middle Frame. His grandson, Yang Chengfu, revised it once more and finalized it as the Big Frame. Simple and easy to learn, the Big Frame has become the most popular Yang-style *Taiji Quan* today. The Yangs enjoyed great fame in Beijing. After 1923, Yang Chengfu visited Nanjing, Shanghai, Hangzhou, Guangzhou and Hankou, where he taught and made popular the Yang-style *Taiji Quan*. The Yang Style is characterized by its fully extended, simple, smooth, light, easy and natural movements. Practitioners should begin with relaxed effort and soft movements, accumulate softness into hardness, then make hard or soft movements properly in order to produce a display of grace and beauty. There are also high, middle and low frames. The beginners can adjust their physical power in practice depending on their age, sex and stamina. It can be used for curing illnesses, preserving health and improving the physique and boxing skills.

3. Wu-style *Taiji Quan*

Wu Style originated with Quan You of the Manchu Nationality (1834-1900) in Daxing County, previously in Hebei Province but now under the Beijing Municipality. He learned the Big Frame from Yang Luchan and later learned the Small Frame from Yang Banhou, the second son of Yang Luchan. Quan You was well-known for his soft play. Jian Quan, son of Quan You, changed his family name to Wu, called himself Wu Jianquan (1870-1942), and acted as though he was a member of the Han nationality. Jianquan inherited the Small Frame with correct forms and round movements. He moved in a relaxed manner and with great ease. His movements, which were continuous and endless, included no jumps or leaps, which made his style more acceptable to the general public. Wu Jianquan first taught his *Taiji Quan* in Beijing, than in Shanghai, where he set up the Jianquan *Taiji Quan* Club.

4. Wu-family *Taiji Quan*

The originator of Wu-family *Taiji Quan* was Wu Yuxiang (1812-1880), born in Yongnian County, Hebei Province. He learned the basics of *Taiji Quan* from Yang Luchan. Later, he studied seriously with Chen Qingping. Based on Wang Zongyue's *On Taiji Quan* and his personal experiences, Wu Yuxiang summed up ten essential body techniques and wrote two books—*Main Points for Pushing*

Hands and *Four-Word Formula—Apply Force, Block the Attacking Force, Counter and Swallow*—which became classics of *Taiji Quan* and *Taiji* Push-Hands. Li Yishe, Wu Yuxiang's grandson, inherited Wu's *Taiji Quan* style and wrote three books describing it—*Five-Word Formulary, Secret Formula for Pushing Hands—Lifting, Guiding, Relaxing* and *Main Points for the Walking Frame and Pushing Hands.* The characteristics of Wu-family *Taiji Quan* are strict body techniques, compact routines, smooth and slow movements and a clear distinction between empty and solid steps. The chest and abdomen are kept upright while advancing, retreating or turning, and the vital energy controls the external form of the movements. This allows the changes between the empty and the solid to occur gracefully. When the hands are extended, they do not surpass the tiptoes.

5. Sun-style *Taiji Quan*

Sun-style *Taiji Quan* originated with Sun Lutang (1861-1932), born in Dingxian, Hebei Province. An ardent student of Wushu, he first learned *Xingyi Quan* (Free-mind Animal-imitating Boxing) and then *Bagua Zhang* (Eight-diagram Palm). He mastered them through hard work. After learning *Taiji Quan* in the first years of the Republic of China, he learned the strong points of all schools, then originated Sun-style *Taiji Quan* with the writing of his book, *The Art of Taiji Quan.* This style is characterized by natural and smooth movements for advancing and retreating. In most cases, the opening and closing steps are used to connect the movements when the direction is changed. It is also known as "*Taiji Quan* with free opening and closing steps."

These five major schools of *Taiji Quan* differ in style and posture, but the composition of their routines and the sequence of movements are similar. Apart from curing illnesses and improving health to prolong life, they are all used for attack and defence. They all have push-hand and weapon exercises, such as *Taiji* Swordplay, *Taiji* Sabreplay and *Taiji* Spearplay.

And they all have the following points in common.

1) Ease and Softness

Body posture while performing *Taiji Quan* is smooth and steady; movements should not be stiff or restrained. They should conform to the phyisological habits of the human body. There should be no sudden rises or falls, no leaps or jumps. Therefore, when you practise a *Taiji Quan* routine once or twice, you will perspire, but you will not pant. Thus, people of different ages, sex or physical condition can learn and practise it. It's an excellent exercise therapy for people in poor health or with chronic diseases.

2) Continuity and Evenness

The routines of *Taiji Quan* are closely connected and continuous from start to finish. There are no clear pauses. The whole set is practised with even speed like floating cloud or a flowing stream of water.

3) Roundness and Naturalness

Unlike other boxing schools, movements of the upper limbs must be round and circular. Straight movements should be avoided because all joints of the human body are naturally bent and crooked. Because of this, some people call *Taiji Quan* "a round sport." Circular exercises make the movements round, natural and soft, and also help to promote the even development of all parts of the human body.

4) Harmony and Completeness

In *Taiji Quan*, both routine and single movements call for harmonious agreement between the upper and lower parts of the body, and between the internal (mind and breathing) and the external (trunk and limbs). There must be cooperation among all body parts. In practising *Taiji Quan*, you must use the waist as axis, and many movements of the limbs are driven by the trunk, and the trunk and the limbs coordinate each other. There should be continuity and agreement.

III. Technical Methods and Postures

The five different schools of *Taiji Quan* under discussion have different styles and characteristics, but their basic technical methods are similar. These can be summarized in the following points.

1. Head Upright

To prop up the head is to raise the crown of the head properly. In *Taiji Quan*, make sure that the head is upright, the crown flat, the neck straight and the chin drawn in. It is required that the *baihui* acupuncture point at the crown of the head be propped up gently as if lifted up by a rope. At the same time, the crown of the head must be kept so flat that a bowl of water placed on it would not spill. To keep the head upright and the crown flat, the neck must be straight and the chin drawn in. But if overdone, this position will make the neck stiff and the movements unnatural. Therefore, in propping up the head, excess effort should be avoided. It must be natural. Once the crown of the head is raised properly, the energy will be summoned and the movements will become steady and sturdy.

2. The Energy Stream Flows to *Dantian* (Pubic Region)

To allow the energy stream to flow to *dantian*, the body techniques must be correct, with the chest broad and the abdomen solid. "Mind on *dantian*" means using the mind to guide the breathing and send the air and energy stream slowly to the belly below the navel. In practising *Taiji*

Quan exercises, abdominal breathing is generally used with the "mind on *dantian*" so as to create a state in which "the body moves in calmness with restrained energy stream and a free mind."

When abdominal breathing is used to increase the energy stream, attention should be paid to naturalness, evenness, and slow exhaling and inhaling. Breathing should cooperate naturally with the exercises. Breathing is naturally linked with the expansion of the chest and the movement of the shoulder blades. A movement is often accompanied by an inhalation and an exhalation. Breathing with the exercises coincides with the body's physiological demands. If used correctly, it helps make the movements more harmonious, round, smooth, gentle and steady.

3. Draw the Chest in and Straighten the Back

To draw the chest in means to relax the chest slightly inward so that the chest is broad and comfortable. This position is good for abdominal breathing. In other words, the radial distance of the thoracic cavity is prolonged from top to bottom and the diaphragm lowered when the joints of the shoulder blades and collar bones are relaxed, the arms slightly closed and the ribs held back. This activity can lower the body weight and improve the performance of the lungs and diaphragm. Drawing the chest in is different from drawing the chest back. Drawing the chest back tends to form a humpback and reduce the thoracic cavity, thus keeping the diaphragm from lowering and smoothing, hindering breathing and preventing the blood from flowing back to the heart. Drawing the chest in is also used for attack and defence in *Taiji* push-hand exercises. If techniques are to be used that will neutralize an attacking movement, drawing the chest in is necessary.

Straightening the back is linked with drawing the chest in. If the chest is drawn in, the back must be straight. To straighten the back is to lower and relax the muscles of the back when the chest is drawn in slightly, with the third vertebra under the neck and between the shoulders slightly pulled up backward, not simply backward. In this way, the muscles of the back have a certain tension and elastic force, and the skin is tightened. As the back is linked with the shoulders and arms, some technical movements that apply force are often completed with the help of the shoulders and the back.

In drawing the chest in and straightening the back, the muscles of the chest and back must be relaxed, and there should be no intentional affectation.

4. Relax the Waist and Keep the Buttocks In

Taiji Quan requires the chest to be drawn in and the energy stream to flow to *dantian*. Therefore, when the chest is drawn in, the waist must be relaxed. To keep the waist relaxed, the whole back must be slightly arched. This will make the sitting and squatting exercises firmer. Relaxation of the waist helps keep down the energy stream and make the lower limbs firmer. It also plays a dominant role in the movements of advancing, retreating and turning, and in using the torso to guide the movements of the four limbs and in keeping the movements complete.

The buttocks should be tucked in slightly when the chest is drawn in, the back straightened and the waist relaxed. The reason for this is to keep the belly full and solid. With the buttocks tucked in, the muscles of the buttocks and waist should be as relaxed as possible, so that the muscles of the buttocks are extended outward and downward, then drawn forward and inward gently as if the lower abdomen is propped up by the buttocks.

5. Make the Crotch Round and Relax the Hips

The crotch is the perineum of the body. The *baihui* acupuncture point at the crown of the head must correspond to the perineum acupuncture point. This is necessary to keep the energy stream flowing freely to the top and the bottom.

The crotch must be round and solid. When the hips are apart and the knees turned slightly inward, the crotch is naturally round. If the knees are opened slightly, the thighs close inward and the hips separate a bit, the crotch is still round. When the perineum is raised slightly, the crotch is naturally solid. When the waist is relaxed and the buttocks tucked in, there will naturally be power from the crotch. Once the crotch has power, the lower limbs become even stronger and the standing steps steadier and firmer.

Taiji Quan stresses "making steps like a cat's walk." It calls for light and steady steps with both legs bent and supporting the body by turns during the exercises. Therefore, the joints of the hipbones must be relaxed and the knee joints nimble to ensure the free turning of the body and easy kicks and step changes of the legs.

6. Drop the Shoulders and Elbows

Taiji Quan requries its practitioners to drop their shoulders and elbows. The arms then feel relaxed and comfortable. This is the inner power of the upper limbs. The inner power is soft apparently, but strong inwardly, as if "a needle is wrapped in cotton." Apart from being dropped, the shoulders should tilt forward slightly so that the chest is completely empty and the back is arched in a circular form. The dropped elbows should also wrap slightly inward so the power will be applied to the upper limbs.

7. Stretch Fingers and Bend Wrist Backward

Stretch the fingers naturally and bend the wrist toward the back and radial side of the hand. For example, in pushing the palm forward, it is slightly cupped before it is pushed forward. This is called empty plam. The palm is stretched slowly from empty to solid. When the palm is pushed forward to the final point, the fingers are stretched out naturally and the palm bends backward at the wrist and the bottom of the palm contains power and protrudes forward so that the power that originates from the waist and the back flows through the dropped shoulders, dropped elbows, stretched fingers, bent wrists and protruding palms to reach the fingers. This is called solid palm. The movements of the palms are part of the movements of the whole body. Stretching the fingers and bending the wrists are actually intended to release the power from the whole body. Therefore, in boxing theory, the power of the whole body "is rooted at the feet, released from the legs, controlled by the waist and displayed in the fingers."

8. Keep the Spine Upright

Keeping the spine upright is important for keeping the body upright and comfortable. If the spine is not upright, it will be inclined and unbalanced. Beginners must make sure that their spine is always upright, whether they are executing a vertical movement or an inclined movement. More important, the upright spine helps make the lower part of the body firm and steady. If the spine is inclined, the lower part of the body loses its centre of balance. When the power of the lower part of the body is separated from that of the upper part of the body, the power is lost.

IV. Basic Exercises

Exercises for the basic routines of *Taiji Quan* include three hand forms and several stances and steps. Repeated practice improves pliability and nimbleness of the joints and ligaments and the elasticity of the muscles. It also leads to better understanding of the related methods of *Taiji Quan*.

1. The Three Hand Forms

The three hand forms of *Taiji Quan* are palm, fist and hook.

(1) Palm   In *Taiji Quan* routines, palm techniques hold a dominant place. The main feature of the *Taiji Quan* palm method is the looseness of the fingers, as opposed to the palm method of *Chang Quan* (Long-style Boxing) in which the thumb is closely bent and the other fingers are kept straight and tightly together. (Fig. 4-1)

Beginners should extend or withdraw their palms naturally and smoothly. The fingers should not be kept tightly together or opened forcefully, nor should the palm be cupped. When you are more skilled in *Taiji Quan*, the movements will come easily. In stretching out your hand, the palm should be slightly cupped. This is empty palm. While the palm is stretched out and turned in a spiral form, it is gradually smoothed out and the cup becomes gradually flat. This is called from empty to solid. When the palm reaches its final point, the cup nearly disappears, the fingers are slightly spread, the palm is seated on the wrist and the bottom of the palm protrudes with slight power applied to it to help extend the palm forward and

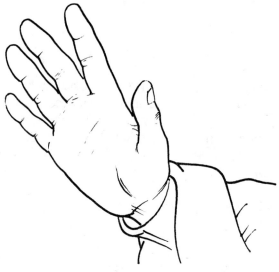

Fig. 4-1

concentrate the mind and power on the fingertips. This is solid palm. When the palm is withdrawn, and it shrinks back in a spiral form, the palm gradually returns to the original state of a shallow cup form. This is called from solid to empty.

Movements of the palms form part of the integral whole. Therefore, the empty and solid state of the palm should be combined with that of the integral whole. As expressed in boxing theory, power is "rooted at the feet, released from the legs, controlled by the waist and displayed in the fingers.... They must be combined as a whole." The movements of the hands should be in keeping with the complete movements of the waist, legs and feet.

In the fixed position of every stance, the fingertips and the tiptoes must respond to each other; the tips of the two hands should also respond to each other, and the fingers should form a straight line with the tip of the nose in most stances. In boxing terminology, this is called "three tips form a straight line."

When the palm is pushed out, its perpendicular face should not be extended further than the knee. If it is extended further, you will lose your centre of balance. The arm should always be bent. Keep a stance of reservation, and change the stance depending on the situation. The movements should not be stiff or interrupted.

The palm methods are generally divided into standing palm, palm upward, palm downward and side palm according to their directions and images.

(2) Fists   The fist form of *Taiji Quan* is the same as that of the other boxing schools in China. That is, the four fingers are kept together and doubled over into the palm, and the thumb is doubled over and inward across the second section of the middle finger. (Fig. 4-2) Although *Taiji Quan* stresses that hardness dwells in softness, it starts with soft movements. So, the hand should not be clenched too tightly. Whether it is tightly or loosely clenched, there should be an indication of cohesion, so that it cannot be opened when it is separated, and cannot be dispersed when it is struck.

The fist methods are divided mainly into fist with side up, fist with palm down and fist with palm up.

After a period of practice, the beginner should learn the changes of the force points. For example, the fist with side up calls for the force to be concentrated on the central flat side of the second knuckle of the little finger, while the fist with palm down is extended with the force on the root section of the middle finger. When the fist is pressed down, the force is on the second section of the middle finger. When the fist is punched upward, the force is on the root section of the middle finger. When the fist is

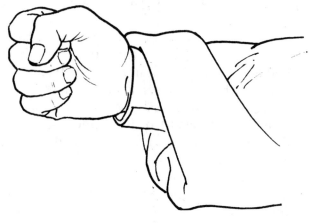

Fig. 4-2

raised with the tiger's mouth up or turned inward or outward with the tiger's mouth down, the force is on the second section of the thumb. When the fist is cutting down with the tiger's mouth up, the force is on the root section of the little finger. When the wrist joint is turned outward with the tiger's mouth obliquely down, the force is on the root section of the forefinger.

Force is applied to the fist, however the force points change from time to time depending on the directions and movements of the fist.

(3) Hook   The hook hand is a hand with the fingers and thumb pressed together and arched downward in the form of a talon. Usually the hook is turned from the palm. (Fig. 4-3). The hook hand is a catch and hold method used in attack and defence, and has four functions—hooking, catching, locking and holding. The catching and holding method of *Taiji Quan* directs its targets at the membrance, arteries and veins, muscles and acupoints. It employs the

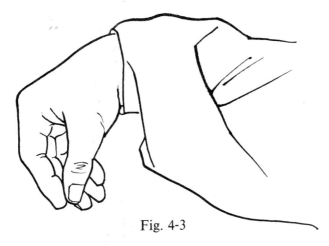

Fig. 4-3

methods of cutting, holding, catching and closing to find the right points through rubbing, wiping, pushing and measuring. It is not limited to twist the mucles and bones, but concentrates on holding the channels for energy flow of the opponent, and taking advantage of the opponent's force to disable him. The hook hand is also a method for training the wrist and achieving finger power.

2. Basic Stances

(1) Horse stance: keep the body upright and relaxed, move the left foot half a step to the left to shoulder breadth. Put the tiptoes of both feet forward with the weight between the legs. Bend the legs with the knee caps not surpassing the tiptoes. Relax the shoulders, drop the hips and keep the *baihui* and the crotch on a perpendicular line to form horse stance. (Fig. 4-4)

(2) T-stance: Keep the feet apart to form a T stance. Put the right tiptoe obliquely forward with weight on the

right leg. Turn the body to the right slightly. At the same time, raise the left heel and place it behind the right heel with the tiptoe touching the ground, to form a right solid and left empty T stance. *Taiji Quan*, in the basic routines of Parting the Wild Horse Mane and Single Whip, use the T stance for holding a ball. (Fig. 4-5)

(3) Follow-up stance: Place the right heel firmly on the ground, with the weight shifted to the right leg, knee bent and tiptoe slightly outward. Raise the left heel with the forward part of the sole on the ground to form a forward solid and backward empty follow-up stance. This stance is used in the routines of Grasping the Peacock's Tail, Apparent Close-up and Hand Strums the Lute. (Fig. 4-6)

(4) Bow stance: Raise the right foot and move it

Fig. 4-4   Fig. 4-5

forward slowly with the heel landing first and the whole sole planted firmly on the ground. Bend the knee forward with the knee cap not surpassing the tiptoe. Drop the hips and waist and straighten the left leg slowly with the tiptoe obliquely forward. Keep the upper part of the body erect, eyes looking forward. (Fig. 4-7)

(5) Empty stance: Bend the right leg at the knee to a half squat to support the weight of the whole body. Bend the left knee slightly with the forward part of the sole on the ground and the heel off the ground to form an empty stance. (Fig. 4-8)

(6) Independent stance (standing on one foot): Place the left tiptoe forward and slightly outward, knee slightly bent, hips and waist slightly turned to the left, face front and weight on the left leg. Raise the right knee until the thigh is parallel to the ground, with the shank drooping, the ankle straight and the tiptoe turned slightly inward. Change legs and repeat the exercise. (Fig. 4-9)

(7) Standing with feet apart: Relax the whole body, keep the upper part of the body upright and move the left foot a half step to the left, both tiptoes forward. Stand with the feet 10-15 cm apart, and the weight between the legs. (Fig. 4-10)

(8) Turning stance: Move the left foot outward and plant it firmly on the ground to the left and forward obliquely. Bend the knees and drop the hips and waist, with the weight shifted to the left leg. Raise the right heel. Turn the waist and hips to the left to form a turning stance. (Fig. 4-11)

3. Basic Footwork

The basic footwork of *Taiji Quan* varies greatly depending on the technical features of the basic routines.

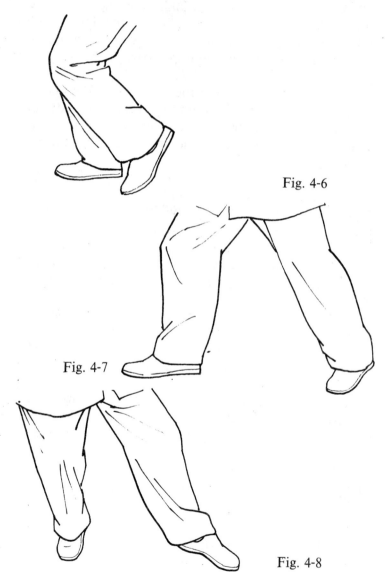

Fig. 4-6

Fig. 4-7

Fig. 4-8

Fig. 4-9

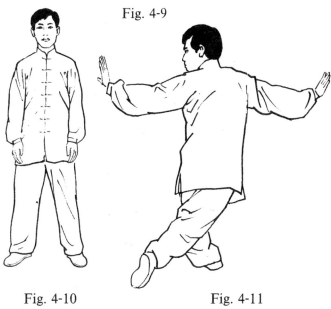

Fig. 4-10   Fig. 4-11

Following are descriptions of two typical footwork movements.

(1) Exercises for changing empty and solid steps

Position of the legs is important in establishing correct posture of the body, permitting movements that are stable and steady, allowing normal breathing for maximum power. *Taiji Quan* requires clear distinction between empty and solid, and lightness and steadiness, when the legs advance, return, turn or change steps. The leg bearing most of the weight is the solid and firm leg, while the other is empty. Only when there is a clear distinction between the empty foot and the solid foot can the movements be steady and flexible and the feet advance, retreat or turn with freedom and ease.

The right foot forward and the left foot behind form the right bow step. In this step, the centre of balance is shifted backward to the left leg, the right heel is on the ground and the tiptoe upward. Then, the centre of balance is shifted forward to the right leg with the sole of the right foot on the ground. From this position, raise the left foot slowly and move it a step forward, with the heel landing first. Shift the centre of balance forward slowly, then plant the whole foot on the ground, with the right leg straightened naturally and the left leg bent at the knee to form a left bow step. Then, shift the centre of balance backward with the right leg supporting the weight of the body and the left tiptoe upward. Next, shift the centre of balance forward with the left leg supporting the body weight. Finally, raise the right foot and move it a step forward, with the right heel landing first and the tiptoe upward. Repeat the exercise. (Figs. 4-12, 4-13, 4-14)

The exercises for this footwork are intended mainly to solve the problems related to the changes from empty to solid and vice versa. During these exercises, be sure to

Fig. 4-12

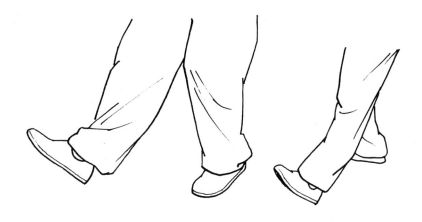

Fig. 4-13

Fig. 4-14

shift the centre of balance smoothly and keep the upper part of the body upright.

(2) Balance exercises

i. Stand with feet apart; concentrate, eyes fixed straight ahead. (Fig. 4-15)

ii. Cross the hands in front of the abdomen and place them in front of the chest, with the palms inward. At the same time, raise the right knee slowly, bend the left leg slightly and stand erect to support the body weight. Eyes fixed on the hands. (Fig. 4-16)

iii. Move both hands upward to shoulder level and draw circles to both sides, palms obliquely outward. Thrust the right foot slowly forward to the right side, with the force on the heel. Eyes should be fixed on the right hand. (Fig. 4-17)

iv. Put down the right leg with the whole foot on the

Fig. 4-15

Fig. 4-16

ground, both hands naturally dropping at your side. Stand with feet apart. Then cross the hands in front of the abdomen and place them in front of the chest, with the palms inward. At the same time, raise the left knee slowly, bend the right leg slightly and stand erect to support the body weight. Eyes should be fixed on the hands. (Fig. 4-18)

v. Move both hands upward to shoulder level and draw circles to both sides, palms obliquely outward. Thrust the left foot slowly forward to the left side, with the force on the heel. Eyes should be fixed on the left hand. (Fig. 4-19)

vi. Put down the left leg with the whole foot on the ground, both hands naturally dropping at your side. Stand with feet apart. Repeat.

Points for emphasis: Keep the body upright. Don't shake it to either side. Keep the balance. Thrust the foot slowly and put down the foot also slowly. The whole movement should be soft and slow and should be executed at an even speed.

Beginners often lose their balance and shake their bodies when they stand on one foot. This is because the foot is not strong enough to support the body. Long practise is needed to keep the balance. Keep the following points in mind:

a. Shift the weight slowly   The common cause for imbalance is the failure to grasp the centre of balance. Shift your weight slowly. For example, if the left leg is the supporting leg, don't raise the right leg all of a sudden. It's essential to plant the left foot firmly on the ground and shift the centre of balance slowly to the left leg and drop the left part of the waist and left hip before lifting the right leg slowly.

b. Balance between the upper limbs   While making the foot movements, the arms should remain balanced. The

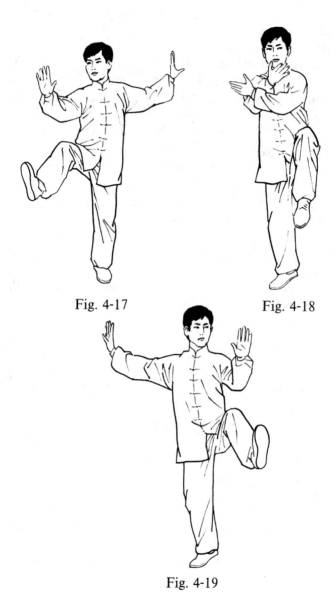

Fig. 4-17

Fig. 4-18

Fig. 4-19

arc and the height of the hands should be equal when they are open. The hands should move apart upward or downward in a curve. This helps balance the body. The hands and feet should cooperate in direction and speed to bring about the integration of hands and feet, elbows and knees and shoulders and hips.

c. Stand straight and centred Beginners often mistakenly incline the upper part of their bodies or lean backward to stand on one foot so as to keep balance. The more they do, the more difficult they find it to keep their balance and stand firmly. This is because they are often afraid of falling, thus they undermine the comfort and naturalness of the upper part of their body. The way to correct this is to prop up the head and keep the upper part of the body upright and relaxed. Only in this way can the supporting leg be relatively firm.

d. Keep the knee joint of the supporting leg slightly bent. This helps to lower the body's centre of gravity and served as a buffer and compensation. It is an important measure used to stabilize one's balance.

V. Simplified *Taiji Quan* Routines

The basic *Taiji Quan* routines described in this book are those that were popularized after the founding of the People's Republic of China. In order to popularize *Taiji Quan* among the masses, the routines already popular in China were sifted and rearranged in 1956. The difficult movements and repetitions were dropped. However, the principal structure and technical content of *Taiji Quan* was retained in these basic routines.

1. Names of Technical Movements

(1) Starting Form
(2) Part the Wild Horse's Mane
(3) White Crane Spreads Its Wings
(4) Right and Left Brush Knee and Twist Step
(5) Play the Lute
(6) Step Back and Whirl Arms
(7) Grasp the Peacock's Tail on the Left
(8) Grasp the Peacock's Tail on the Right
(9) Single Whip
(10) Wave Hands Like Clouds
(11) Single Whip
(12) Pat Horse from on High
(13) Kick with Right Heel
(14) Strike Opponent's Ears with Both Fists
(15) Turn and Kick with Left Heel
(16) Push Down and Stand on Left Leg
(17) Push Down and Stand on Right Leg
(18) Shuttle Back and Forth
(19) Needle at the Sea Bottom

(20) Flash Arms
(21) Turn Body and Punch
(22) Close Up
(23) Cross Hands
(24) Finishing Form

2. Descriptions

(1) Starting Form

i. Stand naturally erect, feet shoulder width apart, tiptoes forward, arms down and hands by the outer sides of the thighs. Eyes to the front. (Fig. 5-1)

Points for emphasis: Keep the head and neck erect, chin slightly drawn in. Don't thrust the chest out or pull in the belly intentionally. Concentrate. (Starting from begins with a standing position at attention and then moves the left foot to the left so that one stands with feet slightly apart).

ii. Raise the hands up slowly forward to shoulder level and width, palms down. Keep the upper part of the body upright, both legs bent to a squat. Press the palms gently downward; keep elbows down and kness opposite each other. Eyes to the front. (Fig. 5-2)

Points for emphasis: Drop the shoulders; keep elbows relaxed and down and fingers slightly bent naturally. Bend the knees and relax the waist. Don't thrust the buttocks out. Keep the body weight between the legs. Dropping of the arms and squatting should be harmonious.

(2) Part the Wild Horse's Mane

i. Turn the upper part of the body slightly to the right and shift the weight to the right leg. At the same time, draw the right arm to the chest and bend it horizontally, palm down. Move the left hand in a curve before the body to the right and downward and place it below the right hand, palm up. Keep the palms in a position as if to hold

Fig. 5-1   Fig. 5-2

a ball. Withdraw the left foot immediately to the inner side of the right foot, tiptoe on the ground. Eyes should be on the right hand. (Fig. 5-3)

ii. Turn the upper part of the body slightly to the left and move the left foot forward to the left, right heel on the ground and right leg naturally straight, to form a left bow step. At the same time, continue to turn the upper part of the body to the left, move the hands slowly with the turning of the body, the left hand upward to the left until it reaches eye level and the right hand downward to the right. Left palm should be obliquely up, elbow slightly bent; right hand should fall by the hip side, elbow slightly bent and palm down. Eyes should be on the left hand. (Fig. 5-4)

iii. Drop the upper part of the body slowly downward and backward and shift the body weight to the right leg, left tiptoe up and slightly outward (about 45-60 degrees). (Fig. 5-5)

iv. Immediately afterwards, plant the left heel firmly on the ground, bend the left leg slowly, turn the body to the left and shift the body weight to the left leg. At the same time, turn the left hand downward, move the left arm in front of the body and bend it horizontally; move the right hand in a curve upward to the left and place it under the left hand, palms facing each other in a position as if to hold a ring. Withdraw the right foot immediately to the inner side of the left foot, tiptoe on the ground. Eyes should be on the left hand. (Fig. 5-6)

v. Move the right leg forward to the right, keep the left leg naturally straight and bend the right leg at the knee to form a right bow step. At the same time, turn the body to the right and move the hands slowly with the turning of the body, the left hand downward to the left and the right hand upward to the right until it reaches eye level (palm obliquely up), elbow slightly bent, left hand should be placed down by the left hip side, elbow slightly bent, palm down and fingertips forward. Eyes should be on the right hand. (Fig. 5-7) (Fig. 5-8 is a frontal view of Fig. 5-7)

vi. Turn the upper part of the body slightly to the right and shift the body weight to the right leg. At the same time, move the right arm in front of the chest and bend it horizontally, palm down. Move the left hand in a curve in front of the body downward to the right and place it below the right hand, palm up, and keep the palms in a position as if to hold a ball. Bend the left leg immediately and withdraw it a bit, tiptoe on the ground. Eyes should be on the right hand. (Fig. 5-9)

vii. Turn the upper part of the body slightly to the left. Move the left foot forward to the left, right heel on the ground and right leg naturally straight, to form a left bow

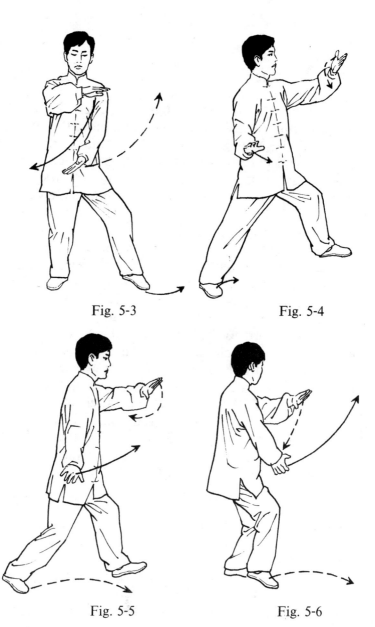

Fig. 5-3

Fig. 5-4

Fig. 5-5

Fig. 5-6

Fig. 5-7   Fig. 5-8

step. At the same time, continue to turn the body to the left, move the hands slowly with the turning of the body, the left hand upward until it reaches eye level (palm obliquely up), elbow slightly bent, and the right hand downward until it is by the right hip, elbow slightly bent, palm down and fingertips forward. Eyes should be on the left hand. (Fig. 5-10)

Points for emphasis: Don't bend the body forward or backward. The chest should be relaxed and comfortable. Keep the arms in a circle when they are separated. The body should be turned with the waist as axis. Movements of the bow step and the separation of the hands should be executed at an even speed. In moving a foot to form a bow step, the heel should land first and then the whole sole slowly, tiptoe forward, with the forward distance of the

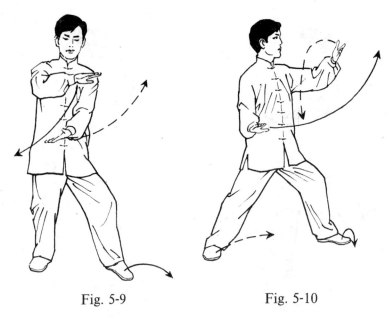

Fig. 5-9   Fig. 5-10

tiptoe not to exceed that of the kneecap. Straighten the
rear leg naturally. The angle between the feet should be
about 45-60 degrees (when needed, the heel of the rear foot
can be moved back again). In making the bow step for
Parting the Wild Horse's Mane, the heels of the feet should
be located on the two sides of the central axis, the crosswise distance between them should be about 10-30 centimetres. (In other words, the centre line of the movement
is the vertical axis and the perpendicular distance on both
sides of the axis should be equal.)
(3) White Crane Spreads Its Wings
     Turn the upper part of the body slightly to the left,
turn the left hand, palm down, and bend the left arm
horizontally in front of the chest. Move the right hand in
a circle upward to the left, palm turned up, to join the left

hand in a position as if to hold a ball. Eyes should be on the left hand. Then, move the right foot half a step forward, with the upper part of the body sitting back, and shift the body weight to the right leg. Turn the upper part of the body first to the right, face right forward. Eyes should be on the right hand. Next, move the left foot slightly forward, tiptoe on the ground, to form a left empty step. At the same time, turn the upper part of the body slightly to the left, face forward. Move the hands slowly with the turning of the body, the right hand upward to the right until it reaches forehead level, palm to the left backward; move the left hand downward until it reaches the left hip, palm down, and fingers forward. Eyes should be to the front. (Fig. 5-11 A, B)

Points for emphasis: Don't thrust the chest out. Keep both arms in semi-circles. Bend the left knee slightly. The shifting of the body weight backward, the raising of the

Fig. 5-11A

Fig. 5-11B

right hand and the pressing down of the left hand should agree with each other.

(4) Right and Left Brush Knee and Twist Step

i. Drop the right hand before the body and move it in a circle from below to backward and upward to the outer side of the right shoulder, elbow slightly bent. Raise the hand to ear level, palm obliquely up. At the same time, move the left hand from left below upward to the right chest, palm obliquely down. At the same time, turn the upper part of the body slightly first to the left and then to the right. Bend the left leg and withdraw it a bit, tiptoe on the ground. Eyes should be on the right hand. (Fig. 5-12)

ii. Turn the upper part of the body to the left, move the left foot forward (slightly to the left) to form a left bow step. At the same time, withdraw the right hand and bend and push it forward to the ear at nose level. At the same time, move the left hand downward and past the left knee to the left hip, fingers forward. Eyes should be on the right hand's fingers. (Fig. 5-13)

iii. Bend the right leg slowly with the upper part of the body sitting back. Shift the body weight to the right leg, move the left tiptoe up and slightly outward, and then, plant the sole slowly and firmly. Bend the left leg forward, turn the body to the left, shift the body weight to the left leg, and move the right foot to the inner side of the left foot, tiptoe on the ground. At the same time, turn the left palm outward and move it from the left back upward in a circle to the outer side of the left shoulder, elbow slightly bent, hand to the ear level, palm obliquely up. Move the right hand with the turning of the body upward and to the left downward in a circle until it is in front of the chest, palm obliquely down. Eyes should be on the left hand. (Fig. 5-14)

iv. Turn the upper part of the body to the right, move

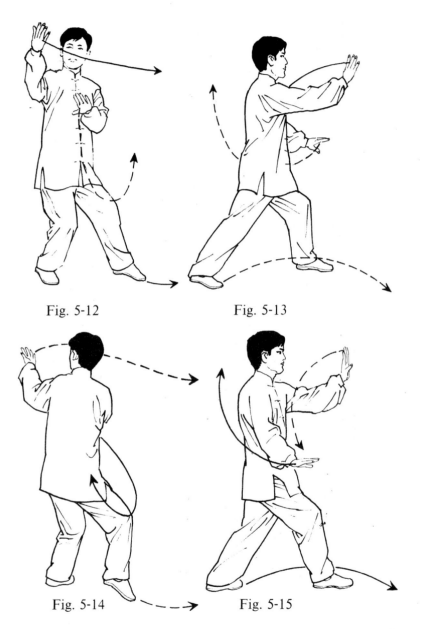

Fig. 5-12

Fig. 5-13

Fig. 5-14

Fig. 5-15

the right foot forward (slightly to the right) to form a right bow step. At the same time, bend the left hand, draw it back and push it forward from the ear side to the nose tip level. Move the right hand downward and past the right knee until it reaches the right hip side, palm down, fingers forward. Eyes should be on the left fingertips. (Fig. 5-15)

v. Bend the left leg at the knee, with the upper part of the body sitting back. Shift the body weight to the left leg, right tiptoe upward and slightly outward, and then plant the heel slowly and firmly. Bend the right leg forward, turn the body to the right, shift the body weight to the right leg and withdraw the left foot, knee bent and tiptoe on the ground. At the same time, turn the right palm outward and move it from the right back upward in a circle to the outer side of the right shoulder, elbow slightly bent, hand to ear height and palm obliquely up. Move the left hand with the turning of the body upward and to the right downward in a circle and bring it to the front of the right abdomen, palm obliquely down. Eyes should be on the right hand. (Fig. 5-16)

vi. Turn the upper part of the body to the left, move the left foot forward (slightly to the left) to form a left bow step. At the same time, bend the right hand, draw it back and push it forward from the ear side to the nose tip level. Move the left hand downward, brush it past the left knee and bring it to the left hip side, fingertips forward and palm down. Eyes should be on the right fingers. (Fig. 5-17)

Points for emphasis: In pushing out the forward hand, don't bend the body forward or backward; relax the waist and hips. Drop the shoulders and elbows, relax the wrist and palm. At the same time, they must agree harmoniously with the relaxation of the waist and the bending of the legs. In brushing the hand past the knee and twisting the

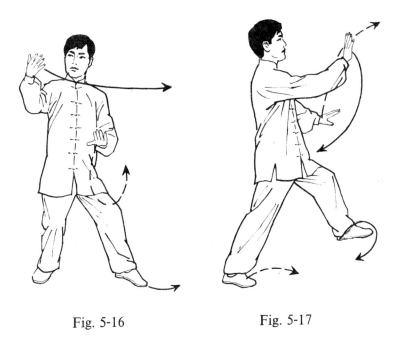

Fig. 5-16   Fig. 5-17

legs to form bow steps, the crosswise distance between the
heels is about 30 centimetres.
(5) Play the Lute
   Move the right foot half a step forward, with the upper
part of the body sitting back. Shift the body weight to the
right leg. Turn the upper part of the body half to the right,
raise the left foot slightly and move it forward a bit to
form a left empty step, tiptoe up and knee slightly bent.
At the same time, lift the left hand upward from left
downward to the right side of the nose tip, palm towards
the right and arm slightly bent. Withdraw the right hand
and place it to the inner side of the left elbow, palm to the
left. Eyes should be on the left forefinger. (Fig. 5-18)
   Points for emphasis: Keep the body steady and stable;
drop the shoulders and elbows; relax the chest. In moving

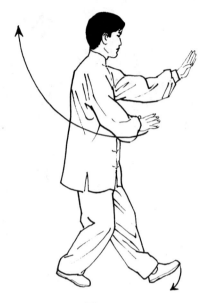

Fig. 5-18

the left hand upward, don't lift it up straight but rather from left upward and forward with a slight curve. In moving the right foot forward, the sole should land first, then the whole foot. There should be harmonious agreement when the body weight is shifted backward, the left hand raised and the right hand draw back.

(6) Step Back and Whirl Arms

i. Turn the upper part of the body to the right; turn the right palm up and move it past the abdomen from below to the back upward in a circle and raise it horizontally, arm slightly bent. Turn the left palm upward immediately. Eyes should follow the turning of the body to the right, first looking to the right and then following the movement of the right hand. (Fig. 5-19)

ii. Bend the right arm at the elbow and double it

forward. Push the right hand forward from the ear side, palm forward. Bend the left elbow and draw it backward, palm up, to the outer side of the left ribs. At the same time, raise the left leg lightly and move it one step backward (slightly to the left). Plant the sole first and then the whole foot slowly but firmly. Shift the body weight to the left leg to form a right empty step. Turn the right foot to the correct position with the sole as axis as the body turns. Eyes should be on the right hand. Then, turn the upper part of the body slightly to the left and, at the same time, move the left hand to the back upward in a circle with the turning of the body and raise it horizontally, palm up. Turn the right palm up immediately. Eyes should first look to the left and then follow the movement of the left hand. (Fig. 5-20)

iii. Bend the left arm at the elbow and double it forward. Push the left hand forward from the ear side, palm forward. Bend the right elbow and draw it backward, palm up, to the outer side of the right ribs. At the same time, raise the right foot lightly and move it one step backward (slightly to the right), plant the sole first and then the whole foot slowly but firmly. Shift the body weight to the right leg to form a left empty step. Turn the left foot to the correct position with the sole as axis as the body turns. Eyes should be on the left hand. Then, turn the upper part of the body slightly to the right and, at the same time, move the right hand to the back upward in a circle with the turning of the body, raising it horizontally, palm up. Turn the left palm up immediately. Eyes should first look to the right, and then forward to the left hand. (Fig. 5-21)

iv. Bend the right arm at the elbow and double it forward. Push the right hand forward from the ear side, palm forward. Bend the left elbow and draw it backward,

Fig. 5-19

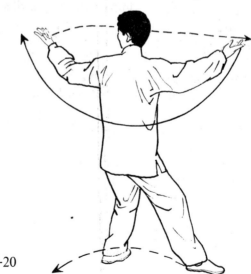

Fig. 5-20

palm up, to the outer side of the left ribs. At the same time, raise the left leg lightly and move it one step backward (slightly to the left); plant the sole first and then the whole foot slowly and firmly. Shift the body weight to the left leg to form a right empty step. Turn the right foot to the correct position with the sole as axis as the body turns. Eyes should be on the right hand. Then, turn the upper part of the body slightly to the left and, at the same time, move the left hand to the back upward in a circle and raise it horizontally, palm up. Turn the right palm up immediately. Eyes should look first to the left, and then forward to the right hand. (Fig. 5-22)

v. Bend the left arm at the elbow and double it forward. Push the left hand forward from the ear side, palm forward. Bend the right elbow and draw it backward, palm up, to the outer side of the right ribs. At the same time, raise the right leg lightly and move it one step backward (slightly to the right); plant the sole first and then the whole foot slowly and firmly. Shift the body weight to the right leg to form a left empty step. Turn the left foot to the correct position with the sole as axis as the body turns. Eyes should be on the left hand. (Fig. 5-23)

Points for emphasis: The pushing hand should not be straightened nor should the withdrawing hand be pulled back straight. They should move in an arc with the turning of the body. In pushing the hand forward, one should turn the waist, relax the hips, move the hands at the same speed and avoid stiffness. In retreating, one should plant the sole first and then the whole foot slowly and firmly. At the same time, one should turn the forward foot to the correct position with the sole as axis as the body turns. When the left foot retreats, move it a bit obliquely to the left. When the right foot retreats, move it a bit obliquely to the right. Avoid keeping both feet in a straight line. In retreating,

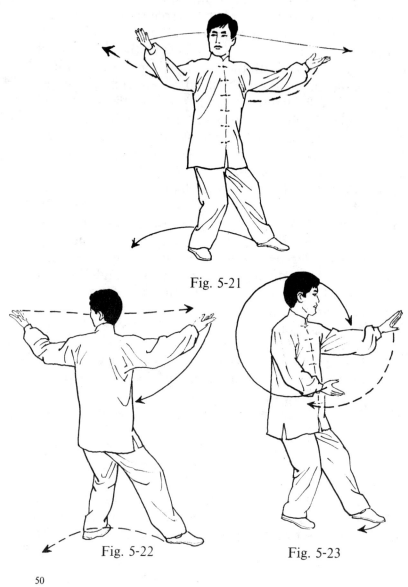

Fig. 5-21

Fig. 5-22

Fig. 5-23

the eyes should first look to the left or right with the movement of the body's turning, and then turn to the forward hand. In the last movement of withdrawing the right foot, the angle of turning the tiptoe outward should be slightly larger for the convenience of continuing the next movement.

(7) Grasp the Peacock's Tail on the Left

i. Turn the upper part of the body slightly to the right and, at the same time, move the right hand to the back upward in a curve with the turning of the body, raising it horizontally, palm up. Relax the left hand, palm down. Eyes should be on the left hand. Continue to turn the body to the right, drop the left hand down naturally. Gradually turn the palm over and move it past the abdomen to the front of the right ribs in a curve, palm up. Bend the right elbow, turn the palm down and draw it back to the front of the right chest. Keep the hands in a position as if to hold a ball. At the same time, shift the body weight to the right leg and withdraw the left foot to the inner side of the right foot, tiptoe on the ground. Eyes should be focused to the right hand. (Fig. 5-24)

ii. Turn the upper part of the body slightly to the left, move the left foot forward to the left, continue to turn the body to the left, straighten the right leg naturally and bend the left leg at the knee to form a left bow step. At the same time, push forward the left forearm to the left (bend the left arm horizontally into the bow form and push it forward with the outer side of the forearm and the back of the hand) to shoulder height, palm backward. Drop the right hand down to the right hip, palm down and finger-tips forward. Eyes should be on the left forearm. (Fig. 5-25)

Points for emphasis: In bending and pushing the left arm, both arms should be kept in a circular form. Hand

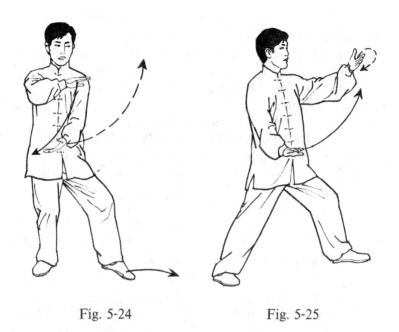

Fig. 5-24   Fig. 5-25

separation, waist relaxation and leg bending must agree with each other harmoniously.

iii. Turn the body slightly to the left, stretch the left hand immediately and turn the palm down. Turn the right palm up, move it upward past the abdomen and stretch it forward to under the left forearm. Then stroke downward with both hands, that is, turn the upper part of the body to the right and move the hands past the abdomen to the right backward in a curve until the right palm reaches shoulder height and the left arm is bent horizontally in front of the chest, palm backward. At the same time, shift the body weight to the right leg. Eyes should be on the left hand. (Figs. 5-26, 5-27)

Points for emphasis: In strocking down with both hands, don't lean the body forward or thrust the buttocks

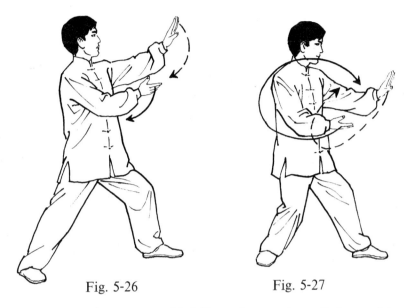

Fig. 5-26   Fig. 5-27

out. The stroking should follow the turning of the waist in a curve. Plant the left sole on the ground.

iv. Turn the upper part of the body slightly to the left, bend the right arm at the elbow and double it back, grab the inner side of the left wrist with the right hand, keeping a distance of about five centimetres. Continue to turn the upper part of the body to the left, push both hands forward with the backs slowly, left palm backward and right palm forward. Keep the left forearm in a semi-circle. At the same time, shift the body weight gradually forward to form a left bow step. Eyes should be on the left wrist. (Fig. 5-28)

Points for emphasis: In pushing with the backs of the hands forward, keep the upper part of the body upright. The pushing must agree with the waist relaxation and leg bending.

v. Turn the left palm down. Move the right hand forward over the left wrist and stretch it to the right at the same level as the left hand, palm down. Move the hands apart to shoulder width. Then, bend the right knee, with the upper part of the body sitting slowly back, and shift the body weight to the right leg, left tiptoe up. At the same time, bend both arms at the elbow and draw them back to the front of the abdomen, palms facing each other. Eyes should be on both hands. (Figs. 5-29, 5-30)

vi. Shift the body weight slowly forward and, at the same time, press both hands forward and upward, palms forward. Bend the left leg to form a left bow step. Eyes should be looking forward. (Fig. 5-31)

Points for emphasis: In pressing the hands forward, move them in a curve with the wrists at shoulder height and both elbows slightly bent.

(8) Grasp the Peacock's Tail on the Right

i. Move the upper part of the body backward to a sitting position, turn it to the right and shift the body weight to the right leg, left tiptoe inward. Move the right hand horizontally to the right in a curve to the right side, and then move it from the right downward and past the abdomen to the left in an arc past the left ribs, palm up. Bend the left arm horizontally in front of the chest, left palm down, to join the right hand in a position as if to hold a ball. At the same time, shift the body weight to the left leg and withdraw the right foot to inside the left foot, tiptoe on the ground. Eyes should be on the left hand. (Fig. 5-32)

ii. Turn the upper part of the body to the right and move the right foot forward to the right. Continue to turn the upper part of the body to the right; straighten the left leg naturally and bend the right leg to form a right bow

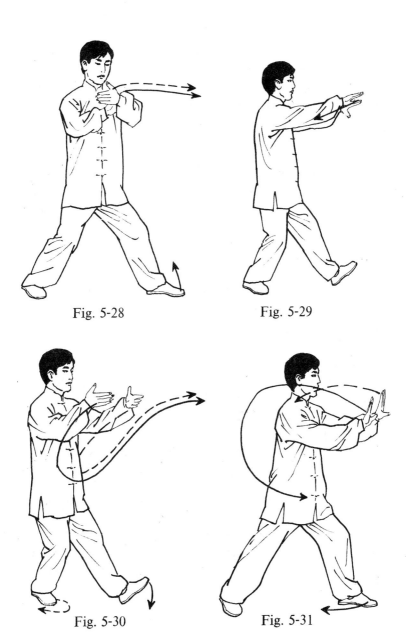

Fig. 5-28

Fig. 5-29

Fig. 5-30

Fig. 5-31

step. At the same time, push forward with the right forearm to the right (bend the right arm horizontally into the bow form and push it forward with the outer side of the forearm and the back of the hand) to shoulder height, palm backward. Drop the left hand down to the left hip, palm down and fingertips forward. Eyes should be on the right forearm. (Fig. 5-33)

iii. Turn the body slightly to the right, stretch the right hand immediately and turn the palm down. Turn the left palm up, move it upward past the abdomen and stretch it forward to under the right forearm. Then, stroke down with both hands, that is, turn the upper part of the body to the left and move the hands past the abdomen to the left backward in an arc until the left palm reaches shoulder height and the right arm is bent horizontally in front of the chest, palm backward. At the same time, shift the body weight to the left leg. Eyes should be on the left hand. (Fig. 5-34)

iv. Turn the upper part of the body slightly to the right; bend the left arm at the elbow and turn it back; grab the inner side of the right wrist with the left hand, keeping a distance of about five centimetres. Continue to turn the upper part of the body to the right; push both hands with the backs forward slowly, right palm backward and left palm forward. Keep the right forearm in a semicircle. At the same time, shift the body weight gradually forward to form a right bow step. Eyes should be on the right wrist. (Fig. 5-35)

v. Turn the right palm down. Move the left hand forward over the right wrist and stretch it to the right at the same level as the right hand, palm down. Move the hands apart to shoulder width. Then, bend the left knee, with the upper part of the body sitting slowly back, and shift the body weight to the left leg, right tiptoe up. At the

Fig. 5-32

Fig. 5-33

Fig. 5-34

Fig. 5-35

same time, bend both arms at the elbow and draw them back to the front of the abdomen, palms down. Eyes should be on both hands. (Fig. 5-36)

vi. Shift the body weight slowly forward and, at the same time, press both hands forward and upward, palms forward. Bend the right leg to form a right bow step. Eyes should be looking toward the front. (Figs. 5-37, 5-38)

Points for emphasis: "Grasp the Peacock's Tail" consists of four movements—pushing with the forearm, stroking, pushing with the backs of both hands and pressing. "Pushing with the forearm" is to block the opponent's arm so that the opponent cannot come close. It is an implicit force that is externally soft but internally hard. For example, it begins with holding the ball on the left side. In making the pushing movement, move the right foot one step forward (slightly to the right), plant the heel first and shift the body weight forward to form a right bow step. In moving the step, turn the waist, relax the hips, keep the upper part of the body naturally upright, relax the chest and bend or stretch the lower limbs naturally. In forming a bow step, don't straighten the rear leg forcefully, so as to avoid affecting the flexibility of the hipbone joint movements. Put the right tiptoe right forward to ensure that the hips are open and the upper part of the body faces the front. As the body weight is shifted forward, hold out the right hand and press the left hand by the side of the hip. The pushing movement must be completed as required by the rules. Breathing should cooperate with the pushing movement.

"Stroking" is to use both hands to deflect from forward to backward but not to grasp the opponent tightly and pull him backward. It is to absorb the opponent's power and make full use of it against him to cause him imbalance.

In making the stroking movement, move the body

Fig. 5-36

Fig. 5-37

Fig. 5-38

backward and downward in a sitting position, shift the body weight to the left leg, keep the heel and the buttocks at a vertical line to form a right empty step and turn the upper part of the body slightly to the left. In moving the hands backward, keep the body upright, drop the shoulders and elbows and avoid leaning the body backward. Exerting force backward and shifting body weight backward should agree with each other.

"Pushing with the backs of both hands" is to use the shoulders and arms to get close to the opponent's body so that the opponent will lose balance and lean backward.

The movements of the lower limbs in pushing with both hands, like the pushing movements, require leg bending, waist relaxation and shifting the body weight forward to form a bow step. Turn the waist and hips slightly with the waist as axis. At the same time, bend the right arm at the elbow, encircle the forearm and push it forward. Exert the force on the right forearm and use the left hand to support the right arm.

"Pressing" is to use the hands to press the opponent forward or downward to make the opponent's body lose balance when he retreats backward.

The pressing movements include sitting on the legs, relaxing the hips and shifting the body weight backward to an empty step (don't lean the body backward so as to avoid the loss of balance). At the same time, rub the hands gently outward to shoulder width and then withdraw them to the front of the chest. Immediately bend the legs, relax the waist and shift the body weight forward to form a bow step. At the same time, press both palms forward.

All the movements should be closely connected and continuous that there are no apparent pauses. No matter how the movements and stances change between empty and solid, they should be continuous. Use the mind to guide the movements. The common saying "when the movements stop, the power does not stop; when the power stops, the mind does not stop" means that the idea of using force in the four movements should be contained in the thoughts.

In making these movements, the body and limbs should cooperate with the breathing. As a rule, inhale while bending and exhale while stretching; inhale while shifting the weight backward and exhale while shifting the weight forward. Only when the mind guides the movements and the movements cooperate with the breathing can the movements of Grasp the Peacock's Tail be executed well.

(9) Single Whip

i. Move the upper part of the body backward to a sitting position and shift the body weight gradually to the left leg, right tiptoe inward. At the same time, turn the upper part of the body to the left; move both hands (left hand higher) to the left in an arc until the left arm is raised horizontally to the left side of the body, palm facing left, and the right hand is moved past the abdomen to the front of the left ribs, palm back upward. Eyes should be on the left hand. Then, shift the body weight gradually to the right leg, turn the upper part of the body to the right and draw the left foot to the right foot, tiptoe on the ground. At the same time, move the right hand upward to the right in an arc (turn the palm inside out) and change it into a hook hand at the right side, arm at shoulder height. Move the left hand downward and past the abdomen to the right upward in an arc and to the front of the right shoulder, palm inward. Eyes should be on the left hand. (Figs. 5-39, 5-40, 5-41)

ii. Turn the upper part of the body slightly to the left, move the left foot to the left side forward and stamp the

Fig. 5-39

Fig. 5-40

Fig. 5-41

Fig. 5-42

right heel backward to form a left bow step. While shifting the body weight to the left leg, turn over the left palm slowly while continuing to turn the body to the left and push it forward, palm forward, fingers at eye level and arm slightly bent. Eyes should be on the left hand. (Fig. 5-42)

Points for emphasis: Keep the upper part of the body upright and relax the waist. In finishing the form, lower the right elbow a bit, left elbow forming a vertical line with the left knee, and keep both shoulders dropped. While turning the left palm over and pushing it forward, the movement should be executed slowly with the turning of the body. Don't turn the palm over too fast or all of a sudden. All transition movements should be harmonious.

(10) Wave Hands Like Clouds

i. Shift the body weight to the right leg, turn the body gradually to the right, left tiptoe inward, and move the left hand past the abdomen upward to the right in an arc to the front of the right shoulder, palm obliquely backward. At the same time, turn the right hand into palm, palm backward. Eyes should be on the left hand. (Fig. 5-43)

ii. Turn the upper part of the body slowly to the left, shift the body weight gradually to the left, move the left hand from the front of the face to the left side of the face (palm should gradually turn to the left) and move the right hand from the right below and past the abdomen and upward on the left in an arc to the front of the right shoulder, palm obliquely backward. At the same time, draw the right foot close to the left foot to form a standing step with feet apart (a distance of about 10-20 centimetres). Eyes should be on the left hand. (Fig. 5-44)

iii. Turn the upper part of the body again to the right and, at the same time, move the left hand past the abdomen to the right upward in an arc to the front of the right shoulder, palm obliquely backward. Move the right hand

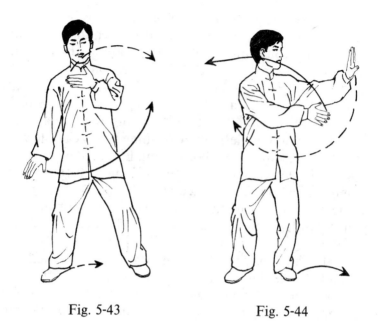

Fig. 5-43   Fig. 5-44

to the right side and turn the palm over to the right; immediately afterwards move the left foot a step apart to the left. Eyes should be on the left hand. (Fig. 5-45)

iv. Turn the upper part of the body slowly to the left, shift the body weight gradually to the left, move the left hand from the front of the face to the left side of the face (palm should gradually turn to the left) and move the right hand from the right below and past the abdomen and upward on the left in an arc to the front of the left shoulder, palm backward. At the same time, draw the right foot close to the left foot to form a standing step with feet apart. Eyes should be on the right hand. (Fig. 5-46)

v. Turn the upper part of the body again to the right and, at the same time, move the left hand past the abdomen to the right upward in an arc to the front of the right

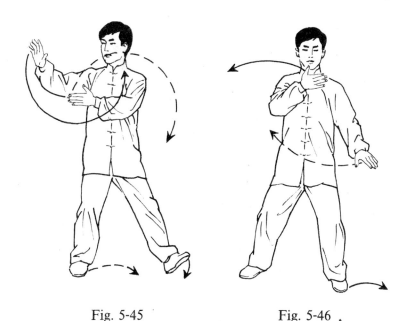

Fig. 5-45　　　　　　　　Fig. 5-46 .

shoulder, palm backward. Move the right hand to the right side and turn the palm over forward; immediately afterwards, move the left leg a step apart to the left. Eyes should be on the left hand. (Fig. 5-47)

vi. Turn the body slowly to the left, shift the body weight gradually to the left, move the left hand from the front of the face to the left side of the face (palm should gradually turn to the left) and move the right hand from the right below and past the abdomen and to the left in an arc to the front of the left shoulder, palm backward. At the same time, draw the right foot close to the left foot to form a standing step with feet apart (a distance of about 10-20 centimetres). Eyes should be on the left hand. (Fig. 5-48)

Points for emphasis: The turning of the waist and back

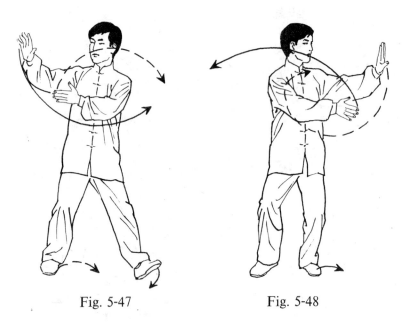

Fig. 5-47   Fig. 5-48

plays the leading role in making the form Waving Hands like Clouds. The power shifts between the two legs, which bear the weight of the whole body. In the course of turning the body, the hands draw vertical circles alternately. The vertical circle moves not in a vertical plane but on a circular perpendicular plane with the turning of the body. It looks like an electric fan with a turning head, in which not only the blades rotate but also the axle frame turns. At the same time, both palms turn outward with the turning of the shoulders and elbows. The head and neck twist naturally with the turning of the torso. Commanded by the waist, the four limbs are motivated so that "when the torso moves, every part of the body moves." If the waist movement is suspended, there will be no axis, and it will be impossible to achieve the flow of the energy stream through the whole body. In the course of turning the body, the waist must be lowered and naturally relaxed, and there is no need to thrust it forward forcefully or to keep the abdominal muscles tense and rigid. The form should not be regarded merely as two hands drawing circles alternately, moving to and fro within the vertical plane in front of the body, or using the hand movements merely to motivate the body movement.

In Waving Hands Like Clouds, the rule for moving the feet to the side of the body is to shift the body weight slowly under the principle "move first to the right when the step is intended for the left." Namely, bend the left leg at the knee slightly, move the left foot a step farther to the left and shift the body weight to the left foot. Move the right foot immediately a step to the left as well. When the right foot is about to land next to the inner side of the left foot, keep the tiptoe upward, turn it slightly to the right and plant it first on the ground. Then plant the sole and heel, in that order.

The cooperation between the hands and eyes is also very important in this form. When the left hand is waved up above, keep the eyes on the movement of the left hand. When the right hand is waved upward, the eyes leave the left hand for the right hand.

In moving the feet crosswise, it is essential to turn the waist and move the arms; the hands should draw curves up and down alternately, the palms turn outward with the turning of the shoulders and elbows, and the eyes should follow the moving hands, so that all movements are continuously connected, and they condition and promote each other to form a set of exercises for the whole body. In repeating the movement of Waving Hands Like Clouds for the third time, when the right foot is moved close to the left foot, the tiptoe should be turned slightly inward so as to continue the next form called Single Whip.

(11) Single Whip

i. Turn the upper part of the body to the right; move the right hand immediately to the right and change it into a hook hand by the right side. Move the left hand past the abdomen and curve it upward to the right to the front of the right shoulder, palm inward. Shift the body weight to the right leg, left tiptoe on the ground. Eyes should be on the left hand. (Fig. 5-49)

ii. Turn the upper part of the body slightly to the left, move the left foot to the left forward side and stamp the right heel backward to form a left bow step. While the body weight is shifted to the left leg, continue to turn the upper part of the body to the left, turn the left palm over slowly and push it forward. (Fig. 5-50)

Points for emphasis: Keep the upper part of the body

Fig. 5-49   Fig. 5-50

upright and relax the waist. In finishing the form, drop the right elbow a bit, with the left elbow forming a vertical line with the left knee, and lower both shoulders. When turning the left palm outward and pushing it forward, the turning and pushing should be done simultaneously. Don't turn the palm too fast or suddenly at the end. All transition movements should agree with each other harmoniously.

(12) Pat Horse from on High

Move the right foot half a step forward behind the left foot, shift the body weight gradually backward to the right foot, change the right hook hand into a palm and turn both palms up, both elbows slightly bent. At the same time, turn the body slightly to the right and lift the left heel gradually off the ground. Eyes should look ahead to the left. Then, turn the upper part of the body slightly to the left, face forward. Push the right palm forward from

Fig. 5-51

the side of the ear, palm forward, fingers at eye level; withdraw the left hand to the front of the waist on the left side, palm up. At the same time move the left foot slightly forward, tiptoe on the ground, to form a left empty step. Eyes should be on the right hand. (Fig. 5-51)

Points for emphasis: Keep the upper part of the body upright and drop both shoulders, with the right elbow slightly down. The body should not rise or fall when you move your feet and shift your body weight.

(13) Kick with Right Heel

i. Turn the left palm up and stretch it forward in front of the left abdomen to above the back of the right hand to form a cross. At the same time, raise the left foot and move it obliquely forward to the left (tiptoe outward). Eyes should be on both hands. (Fig. 5-52)

ii. Shift the body weight forward and straighten the right foot naturally, with the weight falling on the left leg. Turn the body 45 degrees to the left and move the right foot to the inner side of the left foot, tiptoe on the ground. Immediately afterwards, move the hands in an arc up from the sides of the body, palms down, and trace a circle close in front of the chest, right hand outside and left hand inside, both palms inward. At the same time, bend the left leg slightly to support the body weight and bend the right leg at the knee and raise it. Eyes should be on both hands. (Figs. 5-53 A, B)

iii. Keep both palms outward and push them slowly upward in front of the chest in arcs to both sides of the body, palms outward and both arms slightly bent. At the same time, kick forward slowly to the right with the right foot. Eyes should be on the right hand. (Fig. 5-54)

Points for emphasis: Keep the body stable; don't lean forwrad or backward. When the hands are moved apart, keep the wrists and the shoulders at the same level. When

Fig. 5-52

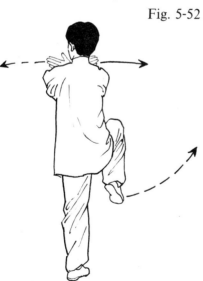

Fig. 5-53A

Fig. 5-53B

Fig. 5-54

kicking, bend the left leg slightly, right tiptoe backward, to exert force on the heel. Hand movements and kicking should agree with each other harmoniously. Keep the right arm and right leg on a vertical line.

(14) Strike Opponent's Ears with Both Fists

Withdraw the right leg, bend the knee and raise it horizontally. Move the left hand from behind, upward and forward, and drop it in front of the body, both palms turned up. Move both hands simultaneously downward in arcs and bring them to each side of the right knee. Eyes should be looking toward the front. Then, plant the right foot forward to the right and shift the body weight gradually forward to form a right bow step, face forward to the right. At the same time, drop the hands, change them slowly into fists and move them upward from both sides and curve them forward to

Fig. 5-55

before the face like pliers, fist to fist, at ear level, fist holes obliquely inward and down (the distance between the fists should be about 10-20 centimetres). Eyes should be on the right fist. (Fig. 5-55)

Points for emphasis: In finishing the form, keep the neck erect, waist and hips relaxed, hands loosely clenched and both shoulders and elbows lowered. Keep both arms curved. The bow step and the body direction in this form are the same as in the form of Kick with Right Leg. The distance between the two heels in the bow step is the same as in the form of Grasp the Peacock's Tail.

(15) Turn and Kick with Left Heel

i. Bend the left leg at the knee, with the body sitting back, shift the body weight to the left leg and turn the upper part of the body to the left, right tiptoe inward. At the same time, move both fists from above to both sides in arcs and raise them horizontally. Eyes should be on the left hand. (Fig. 5-56)

ii. Shift the body weight again to the right leg and withdraw the left foot to the inner side of the right foot, tiptoe on the ground. At the same time, change the hands into palms and close them in curves from the outer circle to the inner circle in front of the chest, left hand outside and right hand inside, both palms inward. Then, bend and raise the left leg slowly and straighten the right leg naturally. Eyes should be on both hands. (Fig. 5-57)

iii. Move the hands apart to the two sides in arcs and push them horizontally, elbows slightly bent, both palms outward. At the same time, kick forward slowly to the left with the left foot. Eyes should be on the left hand. (Fig. 5-58)

Points for emphasis: Keep the body stable. Don't lean forward or backward. In pushing the hands outward, keep the wrists and the shoulders at the same level. In kicking, bend the right leg slightly, left tiptoe backward, and exert the force to the heel. Hand pushing and kicking should agree with each other harmoniously. Keep left arm and left leg on a vertical line.

(16) Push Down and Stand on Left Leg

i. Withdraw the left leg and bend it horizontally. Turn the upper part of the body slightly to the right. Change the right palm into a hook hand, move the left palm upward and to the right in a curve and drop it down to stand in front of the right shoulder, palm outward. Eyes should be on the right hand. Then, bend the right leg slowly to a squating position and stretch the left leg from inside to the left side to form a left crouch stance. Drop the left hand down (palm outward) and move it to the left downward and then forward from the inner side of the left

Fig. 5-56

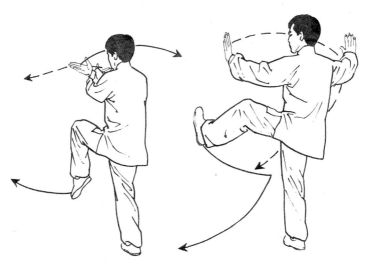

Fig. 5-57　　　　　　　　Fig. 5-58

Fig. 5-59A

Fig. 5-59B

leg. Eyes should be on the left hand. (Figs. 5-59 A, B)

Points for emphasis: In the full squating position, don't lean the upper part of the body forward to much. Keep the left leg straight, left tiptoe inward. Place the left tiptoe and right heel on the central axis.

ii. Shift the body weight forward and pivot on the left heel, tiptoe turned outward as much as possible. Bend the left leg forward and kick backward with the right leg, right tiptoe inward. Turn the upper part of the body slightly to the left and raise it forward. At the same time, continue to stretch the left arm forward (standing palm), palm forward. Drop the right hook hand down, hook backward. Eyes should be on the left hand. (Fig. 5-60)

iii. Continue to move the body forward, with the weight on the left leg. Keep the body erect to support the body weight. Raise the right leg slowly and bend it horizontally to stand on the left leg. At the same time, change the right hook hand into a palm and move it from back below and along the outer side of the right leg and wave it forward in an arc. Bend the arm and put it vertically above the right leg, elbow and knee on a vertical line, palm to the left and fingertips up. Drop the left hand down by the left hip, palm down and fingertips forward. Eyes should be on the right hand. (Fig. 5-61)

Points for emphasis: Keep the upper part of the body upright and bend the standing leg slightly. The tiptoe is naturally down when the right leg is raised up.

(17) Push Down and Stand on Right Leg

i. Plant the right foot in front of the left foot, sole on the ground. Then, pivot the left foot on its ball and turn the body 45 degrees to the left. At the same time, raise the left hand backward horizontally and change it into a hook hand; move the right palm in an arc to the left side with the turning of the body and place it vertically before the

Fig. 5-60

Fig. 5-61

left shoulder, palm obliquely backward. Bend the left leg at the knee slowly to a squat. Stretch the right leg from inward to the right side (slightly backward) to form a right crouch step. Drop the right hand downward to the right and move it forward along the inner side of the right leg. Eyes should be on the right hand. (Fig. 5-62)

ii. Shift the body weight forward and pivot on the right heel, tiptoe turned outward as much as possible. Bend the right leg forward and kick backward with the left leg, left tiptoe inward. Turn the upper part of the body slightly to the right and raise it forward. At the same time, continue to stretch the right arm forward (standing palm), palm to the left. Drop the left hook hand down and change it into a palm, palm backward. Eyes should be on the right hand. (Fig. 5-63)

iii. Continue to move the body forward, shift the weight to the right leg, raise the left leg slowly and bend it horizontally to stand on the right leg. At the same time, wave the left hand from back below forward in an arc along the outer side of the left leg; bend the arm and place it above the left leg, elbow and knee forming a vertical line, palm to the right. Drop the right hand down by the right hipside, palm down, fingertips forward. Eyes should be on the left hand. (Fig. 5-64)

Points for emphasis: Raise the right tiptoe a bit after it touches the ground, then crouch and shift the weight from the left leg to the right leg. Keep the upper part of the body upright, and bend the standing leg slightly. The tiptoe must be naturally down when the left leg is raised.
(18) Shuttle Back and Forth

i. Turn the body slightly to the left and plant the left foot forward, tiptoe outward and upward. At the same time, place the hands before the chest in a position as if to hold a ball (left hand above and right hand below). Eyes

Fig. 5-62

Fig. 5-63

Fig. 5-64

should be on the left forearm. (Fig. 5-65)

ii. Plant the left foot on the ground, withdraw the right foot to the inner side of the left foot, tiptoe on the ground, turn the body to the right and move the right foot forward to the right, leg bent, to form a right bow step. At the same time, raise the right hand upward from before the face; turn the palm and rest it in front of the right forehead, palm obliquely up. Move the left hand first downward on the left side and then past the front of the body and push it forward in an arc to the height of the nose tip, palm forward. Eyes should be on the left hand. (Figs. 5-66, 5-67)

iii. Shift the body weight slightly backward, right tiptoe outward, and immediately afterwards shift the body weight to the right leg, with the left foot following behind

Fig. 5-65

Fig. 5-66

Fig. 5-67

Fig. 5-68

and stopping by the forward part of the inner side of the right foot, tiptoe on the ground. At the same time, move the left hand downward on the left side, past the abdomen in an arc, and backward to join the other hand in front of the right chest in a position as if to hold a ball (right hand above and left hand below). Eyes should be on the right forearm. (Fig. 5-68)

iv. Turn the body to the left, move the left foot forward to the left and bend the leg at the knee to form a left bow step. At the same time, raise the left hand up from before the face, turn the palm and rest it in front of the left forehead, palm obliquely up. Move the right hand past the front of the body in an arc and push it forward to the height of the nose tip, palm forward. Eyes should be on the right hand. (Fig. 5-69)

Points for emphasis: In finishing the form, turn the face obliquely forward. After pushing the hand, don't lean

Fig. 5-69

the upper part of the body forward. When raising the
hands be sure not to raise the shoulders. The hands lifting
and pushing should agree harmoniously with legs bending
and waist relaxing. In making the bow step, the crosswise
distance between the heels should be about 30 centimetres.
(19) Needle at the Sea Bottom
    Move the right foot half a step forward behind the left
foot, shift the body weight to the right leg and move the
left foot slightly forward, tiptoe on the ground, to form a
left empty step. At the same time, turn the body slightly
to the right, move the right hand downward past the front
of the body backward and upward to the front of the ear
above the shoulder. Then, move the right hand with the
turning of the body to the left and thrust it obliquely down
forward from the ear side, palm to the left and the
fingertips obliquely down. At the same time, move the left

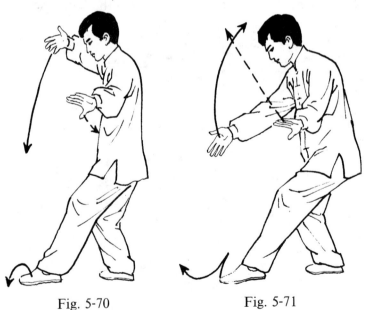

Fig. 5-70   Fig. 5-71

hand forward and downward in an arc and drop it by the left hip, palm down and fingertips forward. Eyes should look forward and down. (Figs. 5-70, 5-71)

Points for emphasis: First turn the body to the right and then to the left. Don't lean the upper part of the body forward too much. Avoid lowering the head and allowing the buttocks to protrude. Bend the left leg slightly.

(20) Flash Arms

Turn the upper part of the body slightly to the right, move the left foot forward and bend the leg at the knee to form a left bow step. At the same time, move the right hand upward in front of the body, bend the arm, raise it up and rest it above in front of the right forehead; turn the palm obliquely up, thumb down. Move the left hand upward and push it forward in front of the chest to the height of the nose tip, palm forward. Eyes should be on

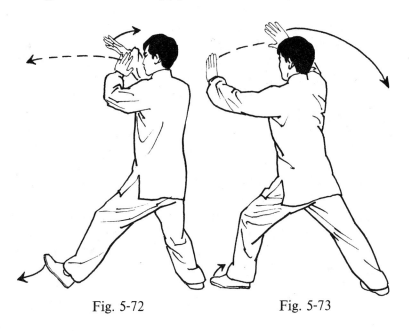

Fig. 5-72   Fig. 5-73

the left hand. (Figs. 5-72, 5-73)

Points for emphasis: In completing the form, keep the upper part of the body naturally upright and relax the waist and hips. Don't straighten the left arm completely. Extend the back muscles. Palm pushing, palm lifting and leg bending should agree with each other harmoniously. In forming the bow step, the crosswise distance between the heels should be no more than 10 centimetres.

(21) Turn Body and Punch

Move the upper part of the body backward down to a sitting position. Shift the body weight to the right leg, left tiptoe inward, turn the body to the right backward and then shift the body weight again to the left leg. At the same time, move the right hand to the right and downward (changed into a fist) with the turning of the body and past the abdomen to the left ribs in an arc, palm down. Raise the left palm upward to the front of the head, palm obliquely up. Eyes should look toward the front. (Figs. 5-74, 5-75)

ii. Continue to turn the body to the right, move the right fist past the chest and forward, turn it over and throw it out, palm inward. Drop the left hand by the left hip, palm down and fingers forward. At the same time, withdraw the foot and move it forward again immediately (no pause or tiptoe on the ground), tiptoe outward. Eyes should be on the right fist. (Fig. 5-76)

iii. Shift the body weight to the right leg and move the left foot with a follow-up step, tiptoe on the ground. Move the left hand upward and past the left side forward in an arc and block it out, palm forward. At the same time, move the right fist to the right in an arc and withdraw it by the right waist side, heart of fist up. Eyes should be on the left hand. (Figs. 5-77, 5-78)

iv. Bend the left leg forward to form a left bow step and straighten the right leg. At the same time, hit forward

Fig. 5-74   Fig. 5-75

Fig. 5-76

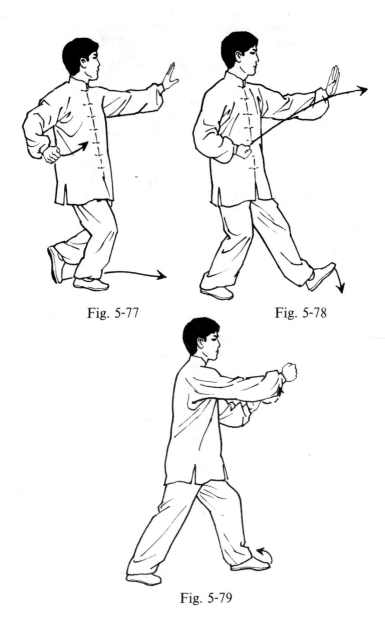

Fig. 5-77

Fig. 5-78

Fig. 5-79

with the right fist, fist hole up to the height of the chest, and grab the inner side of the right forearm with the left palm, palm to the right and fingers up. Eyes should be on the right fist. (Fig. 5-79)

Points for emphasis: Don't clench the right hand too tightly. When withdrawing the right fist, spin the forearm inward slowly in an arc, then spin it outward and rest it by the waist side, heart of the fist up. When hitting forward, extend the right shoulder forward slightly, drop the shoulders and elbow and bend the right arm slightly. In forming the bow step, the crosswise distance between the feet should be no more than 10 centimetres.

(22) Close Up

i. Stretch the left palm forward from under the right wrist, palm up; change the right fist into a palm, turn both palms gradually up, move them apart slowly and withdraw them. At the same time, move the body backward to a sitting position, left tiptoe upward, and shift the body weight to the right leg. Eyes should look toward the front. (Fig. 5-80)

ii. Withdraw both hands to the front of the chest and turn the palms, both palms forward. Move the hands downward, past the abdomen and upward again, and push them forward in an arc, wrists at shoulder height. At the same time, straighten the right leg and bend the left leg forward to form a left bow step. Eyes should look toward the front. (Figs. 5-81, 5-82)

Points for emphasis: When sitting back, avoid leaning backward and thrusting the buttocks forward. When withdrawing the arms, relax the shoulders and elbows slightly instead of withdrawing them straight. The breadth between the hands pushed out should not be greater than shoulder width.

(23) Cross Hands

Fig. 5-80

Fig. 5-81

Fig. 5-82

i. Bend the knees and sit back; shift the body weight to the right leg, left tiptoe inward, and turn the body to the right. At the same time, move the right hand with the turning of the body to the right horizontally to the right in an arc. Raise both arms to both sides horizontally, palms outward, elbows slightly bent. At the same time, move the right tiptoe slightly outward with the turning of the body to form a right side bow step. Eyes should be on the right hand. (Figs. 5-83, 5-84)

ii. Shift the body weight slowly to the left leg, right tiptoe inward, and withdraw it to the left immediately, the distance between the feet being shoulder width. Straighten the legs gradually to form a standing step with feet apart. At the same time, move both hands downward, past the abdomen and upward in an arc to cross in front of the chest, both arms bent in curves, wrists at shoulder height, right hand outside, to form cross hands, both palms inward. Eyes should be on the palms. (Fig. 5-85)

Points for emphasis: Don't lean the upper part of the body forward when the hands are moved apart and together. When standing, keep the body naturally upright, raise the head slightly and drop the chin a bit. In forming the cross hands, keep the arms smooth and comfortable and drop the shoulders and elbows.

(24) Finishing Form

Turn both palms over, palms down. Drop both arms down slowly to both sides of the body. Stand naturally. Eyes should look toward the front. (Figs. 5-86, 5-87, 5-88)

Points for emphasis: When moving the hands apart and dropping them, be sure that the whole body is relaxed. At the same time, the energy stream flows slowly down (exhaling becomes slightly longer). After breathing becomes stable, withdraw the left foot to the right foot and then take a short walk.

Fig. 5-83

Fig. 5-84

Fig. 5-85

92

Fig. 5-86

Fig. 5-87

Fig. 5-88

93

VI. How to Practise *Taiji Quan*

It is not difficult to practise the basics of *Taiji Quan,* however, the endeavor requires painstaking effort and a good understanding before one can become skilled in the practice. Following are some points for beginners:

1. Even Speed

The simplified forms of *Taiji Quan* described in this book originated mainly from the Yang Style. It calls for even speed. Beginners should do the exercises slowly in all movements in order to appreciate the essentials. They should be done at an even speed from start to finish. As skill develops, increased speed follows. The time needed for this set of *Taiji Quan* is four to six minutes.

2. Free Choice Between Different Frames

Body height is not a significant factor in practising *Taiji Quan.* For young and strong people, the frame should be low. Older and less mobile people may choose the high frame. The height of the whole frame should be decided from the starting form. All but some special movements, like push down and stand on one leg, should be kept at the same height.

3. Connections Between Forms

Taiji Quan exercises must be practised continuously. Change of forms means the end of the previous form and the beginning of the connecting form. Beginners should avoid pauses or "discontinuation of power" during the connections, but there should be no hasty changes. *Taiji Quan* exercises and connections of movements are quite natural. Attention should be paid to the parts of the body and the directions of movements. The changes should be both steady and fluid.

4. Single Movements and Routines

Taiji Quan is composed of many single movements and forms. The movements have both generalities and peculiarities. The basis for grasping the whole set of *Taiji Quan* is to understand the technical requirements of every movement. Therefore, the principal forms (such as Wave Hands like Clouds, Single Whip, Grasp Peacock's Tail) should be practised repeatedly so as to make them perfect. Practice of the whole set is essential to get a firm grasp of the inherent rules and to stregnthen the continuity. Ideally, the principal forms and unfamiliar movmenets should be practised three to five times, then the whole set once or twice every day. Of course, the more often you practise, the better.

5. Inherent Awaneness

Taiji Quan is a sport combining form and mind. According to boxing theory. "Form is the body, mind is the application." Expressed in a common metaphor, form is the glass, mind is the wine filling it. Without wine, there is nothing in the glass. Beginners should first get to know the special features of using the mind in the whole set of *Taiji Quan*, that is, naturalness without overstress on the mind, but not looseness. Second, beginners should understand the purpose of every form and every movement and combine mind with form during practice. For example, in doing the exercise of Crane Spreads Its Wings, beginners should imitate a white crane in its perching posture in the eternal form and, at the same time, imagine the gentleness and liveliness of the bird. In this way, they will gradually deepen their understanding of the concept of *Taiji Quan*.

6. How to Handle Contradictions

"*Taiji*" is a harmonious method of balance. *Taiji Quan* skillfully handles the different pairs of opposites in the movement and thus achieves a high degree of unity. For example, advance and retreat, left and right, is always "retreat first when you intend to advance" and "first right when you mean left," so that retreat is advance and left is right. Take relaxation and uprightness as another example: you have to be sure that there is uprightness in looseness and there is looseness in uprightness. When it is upright, it is not tight; when it is loose, it is not lax. The third example is the relationship between bent and straight. All movements in *Taiji Quan* are curved movements and should not be restrained. The joints should not be bent too much, this means that "there is straightness in the bend." Understanding the methods of handling the contradictions in *Taiji Quan* is practice in combining its theory and techniques.

7. Basic Skills not to Be Neglected

The hand forms, stances and footwork changes are the basic skills used in all movements from beginning to end. Therefore, these basic skills must be practised often. Every hand form or stance is related to the whole movement. They are often the "centre of balance" when a movement is completed. Changes in footwork embody the "empty and solid" relations of *Taiji Quan* and they are the transitional connections from the individual parts to the whole. When footwork changes nimbly, the body movements become light, and the feet become so firm they seem "rooted." If the footwork is heavy, it is difficult to practise *Taiji Quan* well. Regular and diligent practice of the basic skills, is essential to mastery of *Taiji Quan*.

Appendix:
Quotations from *Taiji Quan* Classic Texts

Heaven and earth form the major *Taiji*; human beings are the minor *Taiji*. The human being is the body of *Taiji*. Therefore one must not stop practising *Taiji Quan*.

In practising *Taiji Quan*, one should use the mind to facilitate the energy flow instead of clumsy force, and do it naturally.

—Yang Chengfu, *Explanations on Major and Minor Taiji*

Taiji, born from *Wuji* (polelessness), is the mother of yin (negative and lunar) and yang (positive and solar). When it moves, it divides, but when it is still, it combines.

—Wang Zongyue, *On Taiji Quan*

Although the body moves, the mind is still, the energy stream is restrained and the consciousness is clear.

It must be borne in mind that when it moves, everything moves; and when it is still, everything is still. It looks still but it is moving, and it is moving but it is still. Internally it strengthens the spirits and externally it shows the ease and comfortableness.

It is as still as a mountain, but it moves like a great river. Walk like coming to an abyss, and apply force like drawing silk.

The energy stream is straightly fostered without harm, and power is bently reserved with plenty.

It is rooted in the feet, released from the legs, commanded by the waist and expressed in the fingers. From the feet to the legs and then to the waist, the movements should be executed with one complete energy stream.

—Wu Yuxiang, *Main Points for Pushing Hands*

If the mind is not still, there is no concentration. Once the hand is raised, you'll lose the direction. Therefore, the mind must be still.

If the body is rigid, advance or retreat cannot be free. Therefore, the body must be nimble.

The force of the whole body is gathered in a complete whole. It should be differentiated between the false and the true. Force application must have a source; the force is rooted at the heels, commanded by the waist, expressed at the fingers and released from the back. One has to be in full spirits.

Be wholly absorbed, open and close with a rule and distinquish clearly between the empty and the solid. When the left is empty, the right is solid, and when the right is empty, the left is solid. When it is empty, it is by no means entirely powerless, there should be a transfer in the manner. When it is solid, it is by no means deadly planted. There must be high concentration.

—Li Yishe, *Five Word Formulae*

If you expect no defects in the whole body, you must first summon your energy. If you want to summon your energies, you must first be in full spirits so that the energies will not be dissipated. If the energies are not to be dissipated, they must first be gathered in the bones. If the energies are to be gathered in the bones, the front parts of the thighs must first be powerful.

—Li Yishe, *Main Points for Pushing Hands*

Motionlessness means polelessness, and motion is *Taiji*. The grinding of the air led to the birth of *Taiji* and then the division of yin and yang. Therefore, to practise *Taiji*, you have first to learn yin and yang, which is all-embracing. Hence, there exists the mutual promotion and restraint between the five elements and the changes. *Taiji*, originally born from *Wuji*, is the mother of yin and yang.

—Yang Chengfu, *Methods for Using Taiji Quan*

Yin and yang was born from *Taiji*, which was originally poleless. *Taiji Quan* stresses empty and solid, or yin and yang, in every movement. This is why it is called *Taiji*.

—Chen Weiming, *The Art of Taiji Quan*

The name of the boxing is *Taiji*. It is the natural movement of the heaven, and the natural opening and closing of the yin and yang. It is not done by force. To do by force is not the natural logic of *Taiji*.

Apply the boundless energy stream accumulated in the heart to the whole body. Although the form and body are inclined sometimes, there is the vital energy flow to control the movements in the inclination.

When there is nothing in the mind, it is very empty and void. Once there is something in it, it is not empty nor void. Only calmness can help it. Foster the sincerity when 60th calmness and motion permit. Changes are unpredictable.

There is solid in the empty and empty in the solid. This is the successful application of the *Taiji* nature. Only when the result is shown can the brilliance of the theory be understood.

Do boxing exercises to stimulate the blood and vital energy. Breathing should be natural. ...readjust breathing constantly and consolidate the energy stream inside the body and pay attention to the *dantian* acupoint. ...move gently and stop silently and move only according to your mind.

The mind must be empty. When the mind is empty, all parts of the body are empty. The pubic region (*dantian*), waist and foot bottom must be solid. When the three parts are solid, all empty parts of the body become solid. This is called from empty to solid.

As to the hand and foot movements, they are all curved, by no means straight. The circles described are regular or oblique. However, they are nothing but one circle representing one *Taiji*. The exercises are done continuously all along, and the movements are executed in silence without hurry.

Boxing depends extirely on the starting form. Once you

get the form at the start, you get the form in the rest.

Never fail to keep the head upright in boxing from start to finish. If you fail, your limbs lose their bearings and become powerless. This is why the head must be upright as the director of the movements of the whole body.

There are three points to remember in practising *Taiji Quan*. First, in learning it, you should do it slowly, but not stupidly. Second, you should do it faster after you have learned it, but not in confusion or out of order. Third, do it slowly again after quick exercises. This is softness. Hardness is found in softness after the soft movements are executed for a long time. This is called softness combined with hardness.

—Chen Xin, *On Taiji Quan*

图书在版编目 (CIP) 数据

太极拳初步：英文/李兴东著. —北京：

外文出版社, 1998 重印

ISBN 7 - 119 - 00171 - X

Ⅰ.太… Ⅱ.李… Ⅲ.太极拳－英文 Ⅳ.G852.11

中国版本图书馆 CIP 数据核字 (97) 第 22931 号

太极拳初步

李兴东　编著

*

©外文出版社

外文出版社出版

（中国北京百万庄大街 24 号）

邮政编码 100037

北京外文印刷厂印刷

中国国际图书贸易总公司发行

（中国北京车公庄西路 35 号）

北京邮政信箱第 399 号　邮政编码 100044

1995 年(大 32 开)第 1 版

1998 年第 1 版第 2 次印刷

（英）

ISBN 7 - 119 - 00171 - X/G·75(外)

01200

7 - E - 2902P